The

TRUST
MANDATE

The

TRUST
MANDATE

The behavioural science behind how asset
managers *really* win and keep clients

HERMAN BRODIE & KLAUS HARNACK

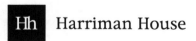 Harriman House

HARRIMAN HOUSE LTD

18 College Street

Petersfield

Hampshire

GU31 4AD

GREAT BRITAIN

Tel: +44 (0)1730 233870

Email: enquiries@harriman-house.com

Website: www.harriman-house.com

First published in Great Britain in 2018. This paperback edition published in 2019.
Copyright © Herman Brodie and Klaus Harnack 2018.

The right of Herman Brodie and Klaus Harnack to be identified as the Authors has
been asserted in accordance with the Copyright, Design and Patents Act 1988.

Hardcover ISBN: 978-0-85719-643-9
Paperback ISBN: 978-0-85719-762-7
eBook ISBN: 978-0-85719-644-6

British Library Cataloguing in Publication Data
A CIP catalogue record for this book can be obtained from the British Library.

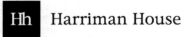 Harriman House

CONTENTS

ABOUT THE AUTHORS

HERMAN BRODIE is the founder of Prospecta, a network that unites professionals with scientists in finance and in psychology to find behavioural solutions to industry challenges. Prior to that, he managed a consultancy that advised major financial institutions across the globe on the exploitation of behavioural finance research. Herman co-wrote the course on behavioural finance for Practical History of Financial Markets at the Edinburgh Business School, and has published numerous articles on the subject. He spent over a decade in investment banking roles in London, Paris, and in Frankfurt, after graduating from the University of Manchester.

KLAUS HARNACK is an academic counsellor, lecturer and researcher for work and organisational psychology at the University of Muenster. Besides his academic roles, he provides interdisciplinary knowledge transfer for a wide range of professionals. He utilises psychological insights and strategies to support professionals in their decision-making, negotiation and conflict management. Klaus received his PhD in Social Psychology and Motivation from the University of Konstanz. He is an author and scientific columnist.

INTRODUCTION

T HE ASSET MANAGEMENT industry is one where, at least for service providers, size really does matter. Success for a firm comes from clients entrusting it with ever more of their assets to manage. A firm typically charges fees as a percentage of its total assets under management (AUM), so its revenues as a business grow together with its managed assets. There are just three sources of growth for a management firm's AUM. The first is through positive investment performance. This simply means the assets the firm judiciously manages are worth more at the end of the period than at the start. The second involves benefiting from a backdrop of economic growth, and the generation of new wealth. Each firm competes for a share of the marginal growth in the global pool of assets seeking delegated management. This pool was estimated at $81.2 trillion at the end of 2016.[1]

The problem for the industry is that combined growth from these first two sources is relatively low, some 1.9% annualised between 2007 and 2016, a period one could consider to be an investment cycle. As a result, the third source has become

---

1   Willis Towers Watson (2017). 'The World's 500 Largest Asset Managers'.

increasingly important for all firms: capturing assets that were previously managed by another firm. Although asset managers like to talk about things like investment philosophy, methodology, innovation, excellence and, of course, performance, none of these things alone can sustain the desired levels of business growth. Ultimately, they all serve merely to adorn the showcase used to lure assets away from other firms. Consequently, every conversation with industry executives eventually comes round to the question of how to make themselves more appealing to potential clients.

In the spring of 2014, Herman Brodie found himself in the centre of such a conversation, during a meeting with several members of the board of a UK-based asset management firm. Once the formal part of the meeting was over, the board members embarked upon a more general discussion about the way the firm communicates with its clients. One board member was visibly dismayed by the seeming inability of the firm's salespeople to make potential clients understand the glaring superiority of its fund products compared to those of its competitors. "*XYZ Asset Management* is able to win mandates despite offering inferior products," he opined, "so we have to work harder on our communication."

The statement was not directed at Herman, but he did wonder why *XYZ Asset Management* might be more appealing to clients. Perhaps it was due to some idiosyncratic characteristic of *XYZ*. This explanation would be difficult for the board to address because, assuming they knew what that characteristic was, they might not be able to easily copy it, or compensate for the lack of it with improved communication. Alternatively, the 'misguided' preference for *XYZ*'s products might be due to the idiosyncratic characteristic of a certain group of fund clients. There too, the board might be powerless to change the preference in their favour. Finally, he thought, if the superiority of the product doesn't seem to count, why does a client choose one financial service provider over another?

In the summer of the same year, a similar question resurfaced, this time at the offices of a European fund management firm. Herman attended a meeting of the senior management team as an advisor. The business was in the lengthy process of implementing the wave of new regulations introduced in the aftermath of the 2007/08 financial crisis. The management team was concerned about the future. While they were confident about the continued quality of their investment products and services, they perceived new regulations to be stricter in their jurisdiction compared to elsewhere in the European Union, and feared a worsening in their competitive position.

The impact of the regulatory shift was already palpable, bemoaned the head of institutional sales. Only recently he had been in a meeting with a potential institutional customer. The meeting had seemed unexceptional at first. It had lasted about an hour, over the course of which the sales head had presented a profile of the firm, its key personnel, their investment philosophy and methodology, the historical performance, as well as a few choice investment case studies. Everything had appeared to be going well. The two representatives from the client firm had seemed impressed by what they had heard. They had nodded approvingly while thumbing through the accompanying pitch book, which summarised in words and graphics the verbal presentation. Then it came time for questions and answers. This looked set to be a simple formality given the conviviality of the meeting thus far. Yet the final question caught the sales manager completely off guard:

> "Your capabilities appear very impressive, but can you give me a good reason why I shouldn't award this mandate to *ABC Investment Management* instead of to you?"

He found it staggering that the client would even mention the name of a competitor at the end of a sales meeting. Clearly, something had gone horribly wrong. Why had the meeting taken such a confrontational turn after what had been a conciliatory encounter? "How do you respond to a question like that?", he asked Herman.

It seemed that the competitor, *ABC*, had some quality that this client appreciated, something that might even have been a prerequisite for them to do any business. Over the course of the hour-long meeting, the sales manager had not demonstrated that his firm, too, had this quality. In hindsight, the final question was the perfect opportunity to make such a demonstration. If his firm did not have *it*, though, he could face a hurdle that might cost him a client. If his firm did not know what *it* was, he could face an even greater hurdle. Herman confessed to not knowing what *it* was either, but it struck him that the missing *it* might be the same *it* the UK-based firm might also have been missing. It would be instructive for them, and for him, to know what *it* was.

So, he set out with the goal of finding out why clients select one manager over another, even if, as was suggested by that board member, the products of the former were inferior to that of the latter. He also wanted to know why it is that during 'difficult' phases in the business relationship, some financial service providers get fired by their clients and others do not, even though the performance of the former might be better than that of the latter. His quest resulted in a collaboration with Klaus Harnack, a cognitive and social psychologist. In early discussions, the pair quickly recognised how common client behaviour like that illustrated above really was – not just in the financial services industry, but in every industry.

Take the example of the gourmet burger restaurant that struggles to lure clients away from the fast-food chain across the street. The food might be of a better quality, yet diners do not frequent the gourmet restaurant in huge numbers. The owners might therefore seek to impress upon the errant public that the food in their restaurant is fresher, tastier, and better-looking than that across the street, using improved communication. But, somehow, we suspect that this approach might not work. The public already suspects the gourmet food might be better – yet still does not choose it.

Another example is that of the worried patient who asks his surgeon about the dangers of an upcoming operation. The doctor carefully explains the stages of the procedure, lists the possible complications, and outlines the statistics concerning recovery times and mortality rates. "Yes, doc," responds the patient, "but what do you think?" Now, the surgeon could reply by citing academic research concerning the patient's pathology, embark on a discussion about the range of alternative treatments, or show the position of the hospital in the international league tables. Yet, once again, we suspect that this is not the answer the patient is looking for.

In all the cases above, the 'clients' seem to need something else, something special, before they can enter into an exchange. Furthermore, this missing 'it' is not related to the objective qualities of the product or service. Instead, it appears to be closely linked to the people who are offering it.

The clients of asset management firms might also require something special before entering into an exchange even though, for the most part, these clients are other financial firms. Of the global pool of assets seeking delegated management, 60% is controlled by institutional investors, a category that includes institutions such as public and private pension funds, non-profit foundations, banks, and insurance companies. These institutional investors are seldom the ultimate owners of the assets – they are typically the 'sponsors' of retirement plans or non-profit assets – but it is they who choose the asset manager. Some of these sponsors also employ investment consultants, who advise them in the selection of asset managers. So, asset management firms actively court both sponsors and these intermediaries. This effort, though, invariably comes down to a person offering a service, and a person on the other side of the table accepting it. By the final step of this exchange – the awarding of mandates to manage a block of institutional assets on a discretionary basis, or inflows from institutional investors into a fund of pooled assets – the client must have encountered the elusive 'it'.

Herman and Klaus sought to understand this missing ingredient by drawing on academic literature in finance and psychology, and combining it with practical experience of scores of asset managers, and other financial service providers, around the world. The 'it', as it turns out, is not only essential to business relationships, it is also a terrain on which few firms seek to actively compete, even though there are few regulatory constraints to them doing so. In its explanations, this book will focus primarily on the institutional investor group, as they represent the most important clients for asset management firms. However, the practical lessons presented here apply to the relationships asset management firms have with other client types, and to the relationships other financial service providers have with their clients.

Many of the people who populate the asset management industry, on both sides of the exchange, are women. However, to avoid the burdensome he/she and him/her, we decided to refer to most of the protagonists in our description of these exchanges as male. Please be assured that all references apply equally to women and men, except where explicitly mentioned.

1 – WHAT DRIVES ASSET FLOWS?

G IVEN THE VITAL role of asset inflows in delivering revenues and growth for asset management firms, researchers in finance have for decades investigated the drivers of clients' decisions to place assets with one firm versus another. To uncover these drivers, the literature has tended to follow one of two broad approaches. The first is a follow-the-money approach. Here, scientists first isolate the firms that experienced asset inflows (outflows), and then work backwards to see whether these firms have anything in common. By identifying the traits that appear to unite the selected (deselected) firms, it ought to be possible to infer the process that resulted in the decision. This method is strictly quantitative and involves crunching data from thousands of firms over several years.

The second approach – fly-on-the-wall – is more qualitative. It involves asking the decision makers at the sponsoring institutions, and at intermediaries, to explain the reasons behind their selection decisions using self-reported surveys. Both methods have their advantages and limitations. This chapter will summarise what these studies have revealed about the drivers of asset flows. The research has not only shed light on the goals and beliefs of the protagonists, but has also revealed some structural issues in the asset management industry, notably conflicts arising from the agent-principal relationship.

FOLLOW THE MONEY

Until the mid-2000s, the follow-the-money approach was by far the most popular. In the US, where roughly half of all global assets under management is domiciled, the large number of asset management firms, and the lengthy history of client-directed asset flows, made it relatively straightforward to collect and analyse data. As the generation of excess investment returns is precisely the reason fund clients delegate asset management, the intuition was that assets should flow to managers who succeed at this unique task and, to some extent, this proved to be the case. Researchers have repeatedly found a positive correlation between asset flows and managers' past performance. However, past performance, or other product-related attributes, were by no means the only factors.

Getting on the radar

A study, which analysed a dataset of asset flows covering some 7,000 products, and spanning a 15-year period to 2000, showed that equity fund management firms whose products outperformed the S&P 500 equity index tended to attract more new inflows.[2] This achievement was a discrete event rather

---

2   Heisler, J., Knittel, C., Neumann, J., Stewart, S. (2007) 'Why Do

than a continuous measure, i.e. it was sufficient for a fund to outperform the benchmark equity index, irrespective of the margin by which it was exceeded, to improve the chance of being selected. The three- and five-year time horizons also seemed to be particularly pertinent for the evaluation of this outperformance. The S&P 500 index, and possibly benchmark indices for other asset classes, seemed to serve as a crude screen in the selection decision; firms that passed through were noticed by would-be clients and subsequently considered for selection.

That sponsors use such screening techniques to whittle down the vast universe of asset managers to a less unwieldy shortlist, is sensible. But this screen appears to have been employed excessively. For many managers, the US blue-chip index was not the benchmark against which their performance would ultimately be measured, so the S&P 500 was for their past, as well as for their future, an irrelevance. Take, for example, value managers. Unless they could consistently outperform the S&P 500 within the constraints of their equity universe, over a three-year period, their chances of attracting additional assets, on a strictly performance basis, might not improve. Sponsors seemed only to consider performance relative to value indices as a secondary criterion.

Performance chasing

An excessive focus on three-year performance relative to the S&P 500 gives rise to a situation where sponsors are attracted to whichever investment style or asset class had performed the

Institutional Plan Sponsors Hire and Fire Their Investment Managers?' *Journal of Business & Economic Studies*, 13 (1), 88–118.

best during the recent past, a behaviour known as 'performance chasing'. Why should sponsors chase after last year's good ideas? One early study to focus comprehensively on institutional manager selection found in data "evidence consistent with a preference by pension sponsors for manager characteristics that can be justified ex-post to a trustee committee."[3] In other words, there was an agency problem; those responsible for the selection decisions sought primarily to minimise the risk of losing their jobs by choosing managers who had been demonstrably successful in the past. One salient characteristic of this was the ability to beat a performance benchmark. Yet, not every sponsor behaved in this way.

On closer inspection, the data revealed that performance chasing was concentrated in a specific subset of sponsors, namely, those who considered themselves to be vulnerable. For some, this vulnerability came from their sensitivity to unfavourable press reports – 'headline risk'. These sponsors would be particularly embarrassed to be publicly seen to have employed managers whose performance was markedly worse than that of their peers. As a result, they were motivated more than others to make the most defensible choices. Another source of vulnerability was the urgent need for solid performance. This is the case, for instance, when a sponsor's pension plan is underfunded, i.e. its liabilities are greater than its assets. In this case, the sponsor can ill afford a subsequent period of underperformance, so tries to select managers whom they perceive to be capable of avoiding a poor outcome in the next period.

---

3   Guercio, D. D. and Tkac, P. A. (2002) 'The Determinants of the Flow of Funds of Managed Portfolios: Mutual Funds versus Pension Funds'. *Journal of Financial and Quantitative Analysis*, 37 (4), 523–557.

Non-performance factors in asset flows

The desire to make selection decisions that are easier to justify ex-post might have influenced another of the research findings, namely that sponsors preferred products with longer track records. There was a strongly positive correlation between product age and asset flows. This suggested that tried-and-tested products aged ten years or more captured more inflows than younger products. At first glance, this would imply ever growing inflows into well-established products. However, there was also a negative correlation between product size and inflows.

Large products were less favoured by institutional investors than their smaller-sized alternatives. This caution might have been due to a recognition that portfolios beyond a certain size are less nimble and therefore represent a hurdle for good performance, or it might be that the fund itself closed to new investors for the same reason. Alternatively, the preference might not have anything to do with performance at all. Sponsors might simply have seen small size as a proxy for greater individual attention, or better customer service, from the asset manager; they would rather be a large fish in a small pond than vice versa. In this case, the data would imply a qualitative element to those selection decisions.

This implication is undeniable in a further finding: asset flows exhibit positive serial correlation. An asset manager who experienced inflows (outflows) was more likely to experience flows in the same direction in the subsequent period. The data reflected cycles of liking (and of disliking) of the manager, which suggested that something was taking place in the relationship between sponsors and managers to encourage this decision-making that was unrelated to any product attribute.

Termination decisions

The firing of an asset manager is indicated in these studies, albeit imperfectly, by asset outflows. Performance, or lack thereof, was the number one factor in explaining termination decisions. However, in contrast to hiring decisions, 12 months was the most pertinent time horizon for evaluating the underperformance. This eagerness to dismiss underperforming managers was, again, led by the sponsors one could classify as 'vulnerable'.

More generally, sponsors also paid far more attention to the managers' adherence to style benchmarks in their decisions to withdraw assets. Those managers who strayed from their self-professed style *strategy* were swiftly sanctioned with outflows. It is worthwhile to note, however, that there was no such sanction for non-adherence to style *exposure*. If managers held assets that were consistent with their strategy, institutional investors seemed not to care how much of these assets they held. This confirms the secondary nature of style considerations in these evaluations. It also reveals that the manager's predictability – doing what he said he was going to do – was more important for clients than his investment aggressiveness. Shortcomings in the latter were forgivable, failures in the former were not.

Performance does not explain everything

Although past performance is positively related to the flow of assets to and from asset managers, its explanatory power is not very strong. Research covering the period 2006–2013 revealed that the top performing managers were not the ones who attracted the most assets.[4] In the long-only investment categories under investigation – US Small/Mid-Cap Equities, Global Fixed Income, Emerging Markets Equities, and US High Yield – the top quintile asset accumulators attracted on average more than four times as much as the top quintile performers (figure 1.1).

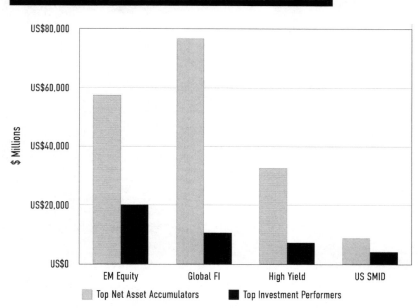

FIGURE 1.1 – TOP QUARTERLY NET ASSET FLOWS, 2006–2013

Source: Chestnut Advisory Group. Reproduced with permission.

A similar picture emerges for termination decisions. If one isolates the bottom quintile of managers in terms of the performance, it becomes clear that these were not the ones who lost the most assets. Indeed, in the Global Fixed Income category, the bottom

---

4   Chestnut Advisory Group (2014). 'Your Performance Doesn't Really Matter'.

quintile performing managers attracted asset inflows during the period (figure 1.2).

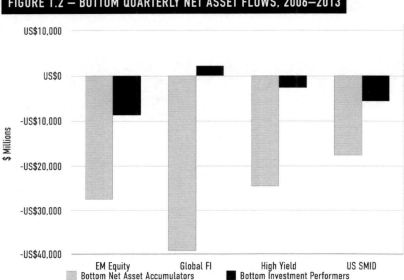

FIGURE 1.2 – BOTTOM QUARTERLY NET ASSET FLOWS, 2006–2013

Source: Chestnut Advisory Group. Reproduced with permission.

The obvious advantage to using flow of funds data to infer decision-making is that it is objective and straightforward. The striking limitation is that this proxy is not perfect. Some flows, for instance, have nothing to do with the management or the product. Sponsors might shift assets from one product to another, sometimes within the same management firm, in response to changes in their preferred asset allocation, to internal or regulatory rule changes, or to personnel changes in the management firm. A sponsor might also need to withdraw funds as an operational requirement, for instance, following a merger. One of the other major constraints of the flow data analysis is that it can only identify correlations in the variables for which data exists, like absolute and relative past performance, or product size and age. Factors that might play a role in selection and termination decisions, but for which no data exists, cannot be captured.

These purely quantitative analyses have also revealed that there are qualitative elements to these decisions worthy of further investigation. What explains the flows that are seemingly unrelated to performance or to operations? Why are some failures sanctioned and others not? Why do sponsors increasingly like (or dislike) a manager when the performance is not better (or worse) than that of another manager? It is to answer questions like these that more recent research has sought to focus on what sponsors say about their own decision-making, rather than about what they do.

FLY ON THE WALL

A recent wide-ranging investigation of selection decisions by sponsors used data from self-reported surveys.[5] To counter any criticism about the objectivity of the survey responses, the study's authors drew on data from a large number of US firms, over an 11-year period, in which several senior figures within a single firm might be anonymously interviewed.[6] The survey's

---

5 Jones, H. & Martinez, J. V. (2017) 'Institutional Investor Expectations, Manager Performance, and Fund Flows'. *The Journal of Financial and Quantitative Analysis*, 1–23. doi:10.1017/S0022109017000850

6 The survey data is compiled by Greenwich Associates and covers approximately half the total universe of US plan sponsors.

questions gathered sponsors' views about asset managers' past and future performance, as well as their opinion of managers' non-performance, service-related qualities. Researchers were therefore able to observe how sponsors formed their expectations about managers' future performance, to see the extent to which those expectations drove selection decisions, and to compare the accuracy of expectations with asset managers' realised performance.

Sponsors' beliefs about future investment success

The results of this study partially confirmed the results of earlier follow-the-money approaches, in that past performance was the number one factor in shaping sponsors' expectations for future performance, even though it did not explain much. A second important factor was their perceptions of the asset managers' investment decision process, and of the quality of their service delivery. These qualitative judgements are collectively known as 'soft factors'. They complement the 'hard factors', like past performance, in shaping sponsors' expectations. Finally, to a very limited degree, sponsors' expectations were also influenced by the recommendations of investment consultants, the intermediaries that most sponsors in the surveys used to advise them in their asset manager search and selection task. The authors noted that neither hard factors, soft factors, nor consultant recommendations were useful in predicting how asset managers would actually perform. However, the accuracy of sponsors' expectations is less central to the goal of this book than how they are formed.

Sponsors' choice of asset manager

When it came to selecting asset managers, the study revealed a stark contrast between sponsors' beliefs about managers' future performance and the managers they subsequently hired. Those sponsors who employed consultants appeared to abandon their own expectations about managers' future performance in favour of the consultant recommendations. Indeed, consultant recommendations became the number one driver of asset flows, pushing hard factors into second place. The authors attributed this tendency to agency problems in institutional asset management. Sponsors, they argued, wary of the career risk associated with disappointing performance, preferred to hire managers whose characteristics were easier to justify ex-post to superiors or to other stakeholders. They did this even against their own expectations about managers' future performance.

The impact of investment consultants

To fully understand the drivers of asset manager selection, therefore, it is essential to uncover what drives consultants' recommendations, because it is apparent that sponsors tend to do what consultants recommend. The use of consultants in asset manager selection is also very widespread. According to *Pensions & Investments*, some $36 trillion worldwide was advised upon by investment consultants in 2016 – approximately half of worldwide AUM.[7] The proportion is even higher for public

---

7   Jenkinson, T., Jones, H. and Martinez, J. V. (2016) 'Picking Winners? Investment Consultants' Recommendations of Fund Managers'. *The Journal of Finance*, 71, 2333–2370. doi:10.1111/jofi.12289.

retirement plans and corporate sponsors. Investment consultants really are the gatekeepers of institutional assets.

In a study that again drew on data from self-reported surveys among investment consultants, researchers sought to analyse the ability of hard and soft factors to explain recommendations.[8] The hard factors included features such as the size of the fund, fees, and, of course, past performance. The soft factors referred to managers' investment decision-making process, and to the quality of service delivery. The results revealed that, although recommendations correlated positively with the fund's past performance, the most important asset manager attributes for consultants were the non-performance factors.

The conclusion from these two survey-based studies is that sponsors tend to sacrifice their own beliefs about the importance of soft factors in influencing investment success, possibly because they are more difficult to justify ex-post, and follow the advice of their consultants. Soft factors, however, re-emerge significantly in the selection process because they are the most important manager attribute for consultants. Whether by accident or design, consultants recommend asset managers that closely reflect sponsors' true expectations about future investment success and, therefore, that sponsors ought to like. Researchers have been puzzled by fund sponsors' continued pursuit of consultant recommendations despite the evidence that they add no value. One explanation might be that recommendations reflect the beliefs sponsors hold, but only dare to express via an intermediary. Consultants absorb some of the career risk of sponsors' decisions.

---

8   Ibid.

Consultants drive flows

A further finding of the study was the extent to which consultant recommendations really do drive asset flows. Sponsors respond to recommendations positively and significantly. In dollar terms, the authors estimate, a fund product whose status changes from 'no recommendations' to 'recommended by all consultants' could expect an extra inflow of assets of some $24 billion. A fund product that is newly recommended (or de-recommended) by just a third of consultants would typically see a 10% increase (or decrease) in its size within 12 months. Bear in mind that the market for investment consultants is highly concentrated, with just five firms carving up a third of the market share between them.

A DETOUR: CAN SELECTORS PICK TOP-PERFORMING MANAGERS?

The studies referred to above have allowed us to shed light on the drivers of asset manager selection. What we have not done, however, is to evaluate how good, or otherwise, those selection decisions were: are sponsors and consultants able to select asset managers who subsequently outperform? We already know agency issues probably exist, which means that sponsors' primary objective might not be to identify managers who are likely to outperform, but rather to be able to justify any choice they make ex-post. With priorities in this order, it would not be surprising if the choice proved suboptimal from a purely economic perspective. Furthermore, these selection choices will not change simply because they have been found wanting in the past. Our pre-occupation in this book, however, is the asset manager. What matters for management firms is knowing why sponsors make their decisions, rather than the ultimate wisdom of those decisions. Nonetheless, curiosity got the better of us, and we suspect the same might be the case among our readers. So here is a brief excursion into the sponsors' and consultants' results.

Fund sponsors' scoresheet

The overarching desire of many sponsors to minimise career risk steers them towards hiring managers following periods of superior performance. Yet, the post-hiring excess returns from these managers are indistinguishable from zero, and sometimes even negative. This result does not mean that a strategy of performance chasing is flawed, per se; the problem is that the sponsors appear to have no timing ability. There is evidence to suggest that the performance of equity asset managers persists. Managers who have performed well in the recent past tend to continue to perform in the immediate future, so there is a rational justification for switching from one manager to another. However, the performance persistence that one could attribute to manager skill tends to be of a short duration, perhaps as short as three months to one year.[9] Even persistence that some might argue should be attributed to familiar risk factors, like momentum,[10]

---

9   Busse, J. A., Goyal, A., & Wahal, S. (2010) 'Performance and persistence in institutional investment management'. *The Journal of Finance*, 65 (2), 765–790.

10   A fund that has done well in the recent past is likely to hold 'winner stocks'

also diminishes beyond three years. Where persistence extends into a fourth year, evidence of which is limited to a small subset of managers, the level of excess returns is already lower than that which prevailed during the previous three.[11] If sponsors need up to five years to evaluate the manager's performance before hiring, the persistence period is likely already over. Hence, post-hiring performance is disappointing.

Underperformance is not the only reason managers are terminated, but it is the number one reason by a considerable margin. Yet the data reveals that managers' post-firing excess returns are frequently positive, sometimes significantly. This means the managers that sponsors fire outperform the ones they hire.[12] In sponsors' defence, it would be unfair to suggest they would be better off pursing the opposite approach to selection and termination. It is possible, for example, that the hiring and firing decisions *are responsible for the manager's subsequent returns.* The growth in assets under management following a hiring decision might introduce diseconomies of scale in a fund that result in diminished performance. The same applies to termination decisions: the subsequent reduction of assets in the fund might remove diseconomies of scale. Any shifts in performance that result from the sponsors' own actions can never become

---

which, because of individual stock momentum, will continue to win and thereby support the fund's continued performance.

11 Kosowski, R., Timmermann, A. G., Wermers, R. and White, H. (2006) 'Can Mutual Fund "Stars" Really Pick Stocks? New Evidence from a Bootstrap Analysis'. *The Journal of Finance*, 61 (6), 2551–2595.

12 Goyal, A. and Wahal, S. (2008) 'The Selection and Termination of Investment Management Firms by Plan Sponsors'. *The Journal of Finance*, 63 (4), 1805–1847.

exploitable by following an alternative selection/deselection approach.

One might also argue that the constant threat of termination helps to maintain a competitive marketplace for delegated asset management by imposing discipline on the fired and non-fired managers (one popular online retailer, for example, has a policy of mandatorily firing 10% of the worst-performing staff each year for precisely this reason). So, although, on average, sponsors gain no advantage from switching, the constant churn might improve the competitive marketplace, i.e. industry returns might be higher, and costs lower, than they would be in a less competitive environment. At least, one must hope this is the case, because switching managers is a costly business. The annual cost of transitioning assets from one manager to another is estimated at between 1–2% of AUM. The non-measurable advantages of the selection/termination process, therefore, would have to be considerable to compensate.

Investment consultants' scoresheet

The evidence from the data on consultant recommendations, and the subsequent fund performance, is similarly sobering: consultants' recommendations add no value to plan sponsors. For example, a portfolio of newly selected fund products would typically underperform a portfolio of newly deselected funds over the subsequent 12 and 24 months. In fairness to investment consultants, this disappointing outcome (which was not statistically significant) might not be due to a lack of skill on their part. Firstly, not all fund products are available to be selected; some products are off-limits to consultants, so they could not recommend them even if they wanted to. Also, the asset inflows (or outflows) to funds in the wake of a revised recommendation could be the *cause* of the subsequent performance. Hence, there is no way to avoid it.

There are some elements of consultants' selection process that are questionable and avoidable. Firstly, as was the case for sponsors, consultants consider hard and soft factors although they have little predictive value for future fund performance, at least, not over the time horizon that is relevant for their clients. This recognition is unlikely to change consultants' willingness to make recommendations, as this is how their business earns money. They earn over 80% of their revenues from providing investment consulting services to institutional asset owners, so this is what they will continue to do.

Secondly, consultants tend to recommend large funds. This conflicts with the choice sponsors would make. Sponsors fear that large funds will experience diminishing marginal returns, and might not be able to offer the individual attention they prefer. Consultants worry less about individual attention because, as gatekeepers to institutional money, they have it anyway. Also, they might prioritise the greater liquidity of large funds over their diminished marginal returns. Consultants have an additional interest to favour larger funds, namely, that they can recommend the same fund to many clients and profit from economies of scale in evaluation and monitoring.

A similar observation can be made about fund fees. Whereas sponsors prefer low fees, the correlation between fees and recommendations is significantly positive. Here, too, consultants have an interest to recommend complex (expensive) products, as they require greater (costlier) due diligence and monitoring by the consultant. So, the size-bias and the complexity-bias might reflect conflicts of interest. Finally, the failure of consultants to add value might be due to the effectiveness of efforts by asset management firms to court them. A top-performing fund might think it does not need consultant recommendations to attract inflows, but a poorly performing fund might think it does. If mediocre funds are successful in currying favour among consultancy firms, the latter might end up making more mediocre recommendations.

SUMMARY

So far, we can conclude that hard factors – principally, past performance – and soft factors inform asset manager selection decisions. For those sponsors who are not advised by investment consultants, the selection decisions are more likely to reflect their beliefs about the predictive power of those two factors, i.e. hard factors are slightly more important than soft factors. Sponsors who employ consultants, in contrast, disregard soft attributes almost entirely, and follow whatever consultants recommend. However, as consultants' recommendations are shaped principally by soft factors, both hard factors and soft factors again stand toe-to-toe in driving asset flows.

Soft factors, overall, are not good predictors of an asset manager's future results, although whether any individual soft factor has explanatory value is not known. What is known for certain about hard factors, though, is that recent performance data is not useful for predicting an asset manager's future performance, at least, not over a time horizon long enough to be relevant for sponsors. Despite this, robust performance over a three-year period is a significant and essential ingredient in their selection decisions. Researchers have attributed this to agency issues: ex-post, it is easier to justify a decision to allocate assets to a manager with top performance than it is to one who, for instance, provides individual attention – even if sponsors value individual attention very highly. The most significant agency issue, however, is the need to be active. As one researcher noted: if fund selectors do not select funds, what are they to do? The consequence of this activity is a constant churn of hires and fires that, by any easily measurable metric, adds no value, but that nonetheless necessitates the continuous establishment of new business relationships.

Those sponsors who employ investment consultants tend to do what these intermediaries recommend, hence, recommendations drive flows. As a second line of ex-post defence for sponsors, this is a prudent strategy. And the advantages do not end there. Consultants' assessments attach considerable weight to managers' character traits, so the effect is to shift the input weights away from past performance, and towards soft factors. This mix better reflects sponsors' genuine beliefs about the determinants of future performance. In effect, consultants allow sponsors to reintegrate soft factors into their decisions without having to take full responsibility for them. The disadvantage to using consultants is that they too exhibit agency issues. For example, their penchant for larger products and higher fees conflicts with sponsors' observed preferences.

The categorisation of all factors related to the managers' investment process and service delivery as 'soft', and everything else as 'hard', is clearly inadequate given their apparent weight in selection decisions. Hence, in the next chapter, we will parse the category to identify the elements to which fund selectors are attuned.

2 — SOFT FACTORS IN ASSET MANAGER SELECTION

THERE ARE COUNTLESS non-performance attributes that sponsors and consultants take into consideration while trying to evaluate asset managers. Their goal in each case, presumably, is to uncover some clues about asset managers that are not observable in the 'hard' data. They obviously find something, because, as we saw in the previous chapter, the managers who attract the most asset inflows are not necessarily the best performers. The 'it' must lie among the non-performance attributes. In this chapter, we will look more closely at these 'soft' factors, to understand what they are, and what sponsors and consultants hope to glean from them.

SOFT FACTORS IN FLOW OF FUNDS DATA

The nature of non-performance factors in the flow of funds to and from asset managers can only be inferred from correlation data. For instance, researchers have found a negative relationship between fund size and inflows from institutional sponsors, which could be attributed to a belief that performance might suffer if the fund outgrows some theoretical capacity.[13] It is also known that sponsors value regular personal interaction with their asset managers, and view negatively the introduction of client service personnel as primary contact people. So the finding from the flow of funds data might simply reflect sponsors' fear of reduced individual attention from their asset manager, or deteriorating client service. Similarly, evidence that asset flows exhibited positive serial correlation – i.e. funds that attracted assets in one period continued to attract in the next, and those that lost assets continued to lose – suggest that there were cycles of liking and disliking at work in the sponsor-manager relationship. This behaviour cannot be explained by hard factors, so is consistent with the view that qualitative judgements play a role in hiring and firing decisions.

SOFT FACTORS IN SURVEY RESPONSES

Surveys are very specific about what they treat as non-performance factors. They regroup elements that concern the 'how?' and the 'who?' of the investment decision, and the elements that concern the facility of the working relationship. The studies reviewed in the first chapter contained lists of 'soft' attributes that comprised the following:

---

13 Guercio, D. D. and Tkac, P. A. (2002) 'The Determinants of the Flow of Funds of Managed Portfolios: Mutual Funds versus Pension Funds'. *Journal of Financial and Quantitative Analysis*, 37 (4), 523–557.

- consistent investment philosophy

- clear decision-making

- capable investment professionals

- understanding of the objectives

- credibility with the investment committee

- the relationship manager

- useful written reports

- useful formal and informal meetings

- the presentation to consultants.

Both sponsors and consultants attach vastly more importance to the first three items on this list than to the others. Yet, the weight of some of the others is, remarkably, not zero. "What can be learned in a 30-minute presentation to consultants, for instance, apart from which manager is more articulate?" bemoaned one sceptic.[14] Whether a manager has 'credibility' with an investment committee, or whether he makes a 'good' presentation to consultants, is highly subjective, yet it influences the decision. Similarly, whether the client relationship manager is 'likeable' is a factor in shaping both sponsors' expectations about future performance, and consultants' recommendations.

---

14 Olson, R. (2005) *The School of Hard Knocks: The Evolution of Pension Investing at Eastman Kodak*. Rochester, NY: RIT Cary Graphic Arts Press.

WHAT DO SELECTORS WANT?

In one-on-one discussions with researchers, those responsible for asset manager selection have spoken of their need to hear managers explain, in easily understandable terms, the underlying premise for their investment performance. Many selectors insist on potential hires being able to demonstrate 'credibility'. Almost all stress the need to have 'confidence' that the appointed manager will continue to play their role, or 'faith' that the positive track record can continue to be delivered.[15] These are precisely the impressions they hope to gain in a 30-minute presentation. Selectors are thus searching for personal character traits to help them make predictions about the manager's future behaviour or, at least, to reassure them that the positive impressions they have gained elsewhere are justified.

Sponsors and consultants also use soft factors to evaluate the investment process, and the way that investment managers contribute to it. Bear in mind that selectors already spend a great deal of time analysing past performance, so they are aware of the *outcomes* of managers' past decisions. However, those managers might be employed by different firms, working within different teams, or pursuing different investment philosophies, than at the time the track records were established. Hence, selectors want to judge whether managers have the authority, discipline and the operational support, necessary to realise their current plans. They want to be confident that decision processes

---

15 Foster, F. D. and Warren, G. (2013) 'Equity Manager Selection and Portfolio Formation: Interviews with Investment Staff'. *Financial Research Network (FIRN) Research Papers*, 2, (2).

are consistent with the current investment philosophies. They also want to be sure that the current investment team members fit together, and that the teams fit their respective organisations. They know the process worked in the past: they want to be sure that all the pieces are in place for it to work in the future.

The goal of this book is neither to endorse nor condemn selection methods, merely to understand them, and to predict their outcomes. It is worth recalling, though, that the future performance of asset managers does not correlate with the soft factor scores attributed to them by either sponsors or consultants, so these perceptions are not always accurate. This does not mean that soft factors are pointless; evaluating the personal qualities of the manager, and the performance qualities of the investment process, is reasonably viewed as an essential part of any due diligence. The problem, if one can describe it as such, lies in the way selectors perceive these qualities. Perceptions are subjective and, as subjectivity increases, so more of the decision-making takes place at the emotional level and becomes increasingly exposed to bias and influence. All asset managers try to appear 'credible' to selectors. They all try to inspire 'confidence' in their investment philosophies, and 'faith' in their ability to realise them. Yet only some of these managers succeed in eliciting these perceptions, and these are not necessarily the ones who go on to deliver the desired investment performance.

WHAT DO SELECTORS (REALLY) WANT?

The focus of soft factors is distinct from that of hard factors in one key respect. Whereas hard factors concern solely the past – product age, past inflows and outflows, past performance, etc. – soft factors are how selectors make a prediction about the future. Therefore, they attach the greatest weight to elements that increase the perception of behaviour predictability, like 'consistency'. Clients want to have a relationship with their service providers. Hard factors tell them nothing about the kind of relationship they will have; only soft factors can do that.

Tell me about yourself

Several academic researchers have published anecdotal evidence concerning the process of asset manager selection, as well as candid comments made to them by sponsors. Some sponsors have even written detailed descriptions of the way they go about the selection task. This literature shows that a combination of quantitative assessments and qualitative judgements is common, but also reveals that the subjective evaluation of the individuals carries the most weight: "judgement rules, quants are tools."[16]

One selector refers to his method as the 'three Ps': people, process, performance[17] (for another, the three Ps are more

---

16 Ibid.

17 Travers, F. J. (2004) *Investment Manager Analysis: A Comprehensive Guide to Portfolio Selection, Monitoring and Optimization.* ISBN: 978-0-471-47886-7

straightforward: "the people, the people, the people."[18]). It refers to a comprehensive analytical approach that involves setting clear investment guidelines; sourcing potential asset managers; analysing their portfolios' risk-adjusted performance; and gathering specific information through a lengthy and detailed questionnaire. Only after these stages have been completed does he envisage any face-to-face or telephone contact with the candidate firm. For those asset managers who make it that far, he reserves his first request: "Tell me about yourself."

It is worth recalling that, by this stage, he already knows a great deal about the firm, its history, and its key personnel. He does not need a biography, because he has it already. What he wants to discover is what makes these people tick. Preferably, he says, he sits with them in their own personal office space, as "a person's office space speaks volumes about the kind of person he or she is." The selector also wants to discover how much professional time is to be dedicated to the product being managed for him. He confides: "So that I can be assured that on any given day they have my best interests at heart." He also wants to see how potential managers perceive and respond to conflicts of interest. He cites the example of the commission rates the investment firm pays on trades, and any soft-dollar[19] arrangements it might

---

18 Foster, F. D. and Warren, G. (2013) 'Equity Manager Selection and Portfolio Formation: Interviews with Investment Staff'. *Financial Research Network (FIRN) Research Papers*, 2, (2).

19 Soft-dollar agreements are arrangements between asset managers and their brokers, whereby the manager pays a high commission rate for transactions and the broker uses some of the revenues – soft dollars – to pay for external services used by the sponsor, e.g. investment research or IT equipment. The incentive for the manager is that commissions are charged to the client account, while a direct payment for the services would be charged

have. High commissions suggest that the firm might be putting its own interests ahead of those of the client.

The request, "Tell me about yourself", would not be out of place in a Brontë-esque novel. This would be in the scene where the suitor presents himself to the girl's father to ask permission to court her. The patriarch, usually while cleaning his shotgun, receives the boy in his study and asks: "What are your intentions towards my daughter?" The motivation behind the question directed at asset managers is the same. It is about managers' character, their guiding principles, their intentions towards the client. Whose interests do they put first, the clients' or their own? Whether selectors justify this query as a need to have 'confidence' or 'faith' (assuming they verbalise it at all), this is a question they all want answered. The selector knows that at some stage in the relationship there might come a time when the manager stands at a moral crossroads – turn left, and the client's interests are best served; turn right, and the manager's interests are served. Both alternatives might be permissible, and both might be justifiable. What will the manager choose? Despite the intensive effort to understand and evaluate asset managers' ability, the evaluation that matters the most is the one that concerns for whose benefit that ability will be deployed. Will managers work primarily for clients or for themselves?

---

to the management firm. The higher the commissions, and the more trades the firm does, the more soft dollars it accumulates.

SUMMARY

If the review of literature has revealed anything about soft factors, it is that they are extremely difficult to define. Non-performance elements explain much more of the manager selection decision than performance. That much is evident from the flow-of-funds data. And even in these supposedly 'hard' numbers, one can imply or intuit some 'soft' drivers. Similarly, not everything that is non-performance related is necessarily 'soft'. For example, the list of soft factors proposed in self-reported surveys, although long, lacks precision. Some might argue that that not all of them are genuinely 'soft', or that there is generous overlap between hard and soft. Also, the list is far from exhaustive. It is rather in the one-on-one conversations that researchers have shared with sponsors and consultants, and in the how-to guides and chronicles that some selectors have published about their work, that the real nature of those non-performance factors starts to emerge.

Before entering into a business exchange with the service provider, clients try to gauge what kind of relationship it will be. Past performance data tells them nothing about that future relationship, so they look for inspiration from alternative sources, like the 30-minute presentation, or even the state of the person's working space. They also rely on their personal impressions of the other's 'character' and 'credibility', and give weight to information that reflects predictability, as this means those impressions will also be valid in the future. Hence, they laud 'consistency' and 'clarity'. The most important trait selectors look for, however, concerns the manager's intentions. They want to know whose best interests the manager has at heart. Even able managers will only be retained if selectors are convinced they will use that ability to further the clients' interests ahead of their own.

3 — THE ROLE OF TRUST IN ECONOMIC RELATIONSHIPS

I N THE PREVIOUS chapters we showed that the asset manager selection process essentially allows sponsors to make two core judgements about potential candidates. One is about the manager's ability, which they do by evaluating proven past behaviour. The other is a prediction about the manager's future behaviour, which can only be done by trying to gauge that person's intentions. The evidence also suggests that the latter is the more important of the two, so it was here that we pursued our quest for the 'it'.

THE LOGIC OF GOOD INTENTIONS

It might appear counterintuitive that selectors should dwell so lengthily on intentions, given that investment success will ultimately rely on the asset manager's ability. Yet the primacy of intent is nonetheless logical. A skilled person, in any endeavour, is only useful to us if he is on our side. If he is on the opposing side, we will not value that skill; we would even prefer him to be unskilled. One cannot, therefore, evaluate a person's skill in isolation from his intent, nor his intent in isolation from his skill. So, although the two judgements are made independently, relying on a completely different set of signals, they combine to provide a unified impression of the person.

Armed with an impression of a counterparty, clients decide whether they are prepared to enter a business relationship with that person, and about the depth of that relationship. This means that to win clients, financial service providers must be concerned about the entire impression they convey – their ability, of course, but much more importantly, their intentions. This chapter will focus on the crucial role intentions play as a driver of business relationships, and introduce the concept known as trust.

THE DEFINITION OF TRUST

Psychologists have spent decades investigating the way people form impressions about others. This has involved asking all kinds of people, all around the world, about their impressions of others, and conducting factor analyses of the results. Such studies have repeatedly revealed that two specific judgements play essential roles in shaping our global impressions of others. Indeed, around the same time the first flow-of-funds study cited in chapter 1 was published, two equally enlightening studies appeared in social sciences journals. The first concerned impression formation, and highlighted two traits, labelled 'morality' and 'competence', as key in our global impression of others, with morality being the dominant of the two.[20] Subsequent research concluded that these twin judgements are truly universal. Not only do sponsors and consultants judge asset managers in this way, but everybody judges everybody else in this way too. The second study showed that these two judgements, under conditions of risk or vulnerability, describe the sentiment more commonly referred to as trust.[21] By this definition, what sponsors seek are not asset managers they believe will outperform, but ones they can trust. Consultants, too, do not recommend managers who can outperform. What they do, deliberately or inadvertently, is recommend asset managers that sponsors will perceive to be trustworthy.

This description of trust remains widely accepted in the scientific literature. Trust is defined as "a psychological state comprising the intention to accept vulnerability based upon positive expectations of the intentions or behaviour of another."[22] Trust is not a behaviour, therefore, but a state of mind. The presence or otherwise of this state of mind when a risky decision must be made determines whether trust translates into trusting behaviour. Trust is a willingness to rely on another party (i.e. a person, group or organisation), though one is aware that by doing so one could expose oneself to negative outcomes (injury or loss) if the other party proves to be untrustworthy. A trustor

---

20 Wojciszke, B., Bazinska, R., and Jaworski, M. (1998) 'On the dominance of moral categories in impression formation'. *Personality and Social Psychology Bulletin.* 24 (12), 1245–1257.

21 Rousseau, D. M., Sitkin, S. B., Burt, R. S. and Camerer, C. F. (1998) 'Not so different after all: A cross-discipline view of trust'. *Academy of Management Review*, 23 (3), 393–404.

22 Ibid.

is someone whose state of mind allows him to run this risk nonetheless, because he believes the other party is motivated to act in a way that not only spares him such injury or loss, but that yields some benefit or gain.

In the context of asset manager selection, we have taken the liberty of redefining trust to highlight the key elements:

> *Before taking a risk, clients want to be convinced the manager is both willing and able to act in their interests.*

Taking a risk means the client accepts being vulnerable vis-à-vis the manager – accepts putting his fate in the manager's hands. The client also believes that, in doing so, everything will work out fine because the manager is not only motivated to act in his interests – i.e. has benevolent intentions – but is also capable of doing so.

Trust is inseparable from risk

Clients expose themselves to undesirable outcomes if the manager lacks either the motivation or the ability to protect their interests. Trust is, therefore, inseparable from risk or vulnerability. There is no need for trust in the absence of risk. The greater the vulnerability, the greater the potential for trust. Trust, however, is more than just the recognition of vulnerability; it is the optimistic acceptance of it.

Imagine for example, that your newish smartphone fell into the bath and stopped functioning. Now you are faced with the choice of getting a new one, and losing your pictures, messages and other data, or going to the store and trying to get it fixed. A work colleague is convinced he can fix it, and offers to attempt a free repair. Do you hand the smartphone over? Your first thought would surely be about the sensitivity of the data stored in its memory, and about what the colleague might do with it should he be able to breathe life back into the device. If the smartphone carries no sensitive data – i.e. you are not vulnerable – you might well hand it over. As there is no risk, a transaction can take place even in the absence of trust. If the device's memory holds sensitive data, however, you would probably wonder about the other's intentions. Without trust, in this case, there can be no transaction, and the more sensitive the data, the higher the trust hurdle. Over the course of this reflection, you might have noticed that ability has not yet played any role. You have not asked yourself the question whether the colleague has any skill in repairing hi-tech devices. Even though the success of the transaction – the repair of the smartphone – will ultimately depend on his abilities in this domain, that judgement occupies a distant second place in your decision-making. The first judgement to be made is always about the other's intentions.

No-trust business relationships

The implication of the above is that financial service providers can still win business even if they are not trusted, as long as there is little or no risk for the client. For example, a top-ranked investment bank, even one whose reputation for ethical behaviour is unflattering, can still win a small part of every potential client's business (a small part of *everyone's* business is still a great deal of business). This is because a small part of the business does not represent a huge risk for the client. However, the bank might never win a large part of any client's business, because this would require that the client accept being in a vulnerable position. Similarly, a top-performing investment management firm, even one whose philosophies are ambiguous, can still attract assets to its developed-market equity index fund. This investment exposes the sponsor to a low level of risk, which is acceptable even in the absence of trust. Yet the same sponsor might be unwilling to delegate the management of an emerging-market corporate bond fund to this firm because to do so would involve considerable risk. If risk is involved, trust is essential. So, in a risk-orientated business, like asset management, trust is a genuine asset – a form of social capital.

SOCIAL CAPITAL

It is only in the past 25 years that economists have looked seriously at the role of trust in shaping economic outcomes – microeconomic as well as macroeconomic outcomes. The resulting research has revealed that high levels of trust within and between firms, and the prevailing level of trust among people in the broader society, have positive implications for their relative economic performance. Trust, therefore, is a form of social capital for societies, and for firms, on a par with other economic assets.

Trust and macroeconomic activity

"Generally speaking, would you say that most people can be trusted, or that you can't be too careful in dealing with people?"

This is the question the World Values Survey,[23] regularly asks thousands of people, in 29 market economies around the world. The proportion of people who agree that others in their respective country can be trusted varies impressively. In countries such Norway, Denmark and the Netherlands, as many as two-thirds of the population agree with the statement. In contrast, the proportion can be as low as 10% in countries such as Brazil, Turkey and the Philippines. Using these proportions as a measure of generalised trust, or social trust, many researchers have sought to uncover any causal role in economic outcomes.

The evidence shows that norms of trust in a society have a significant impact on aggregate economic activity.[24] GDP growth, for example, tends to be higher in countries where people trust each other more. This is mostly due to the higher incidence of investment (as a proportion of GDP) in those countries. High-trust countries tend to invest more in their human capital, too, as school enrolment and attainment is positively correlated with trust. Social trust is also related to economic equality, happiness, health and tolerance towards minorities.[25,26] Even differences in political economics across the world have been attributed to

---

23 The World Values Survey (www.worldvaluessurvey.org) is a global network of social scientists studying changing values and their impact on social and political life, led by an international team of scholars, with the WVS Association and WVSA Secretariat headquartered in Vienna, Austria.

24 Knack, S. and Keefer, P. (1997) 'Does Social Capital Have an Economic Payoff? A Cross-Country Investigation'. *The Quarterly Journal of Economics*, 112 (4), 1251–1288.

25 Rothstein, B. and Uslaner, E. M. (2005) 'All for All: Equality, Corruption, and Social Trust'. *World Politics*, Volume 58 (1), 41–72.

26 Uslaner, E. M. (2002) *The Moral Foundations of Trust*. New York: Cambridge University Press.

differences in countries' underlying social trust.[27] Countries with elevated levels of social trust tend to be more democratic, and have better-performing democratic institutions.

In comments following the publication of the 2015 World Values Survey, Dr David Halpern, CEO of the UK's Behavioural Insights Team, summarised:

> "Levels of social trust, averaged across a country, predict national economic growth as powerfully as financial and physical capital, and more powerfully than skill levels – over which every government in the world worries about incessantly. It is also associated with many other non-economic outcomes, such as life satisfaction (positively) and suicide (negatively). In short, it's not much fun living in a place where you don't think most other people can be trusted. Low trust implies a society where you have to keep an eye over your shoulder; where deals need lawyers instead of handshakes; where you don't see the point of paying your tax or recycling your rubbish (since you doubt your neighbour will do so); and where you employ your cousin or your brother-in-law to work for you rather than a stranger who would probably be much better at the job."

Trust and market efficiency

In the US, the World Values Survey divides respondents into ten geographical regions.[28] This breakdown reveals meaningful

---

27 Fukuyama, F. (1995) *Trust: The social virtues and the creation of prosperity*. New York: Free Press.

28 New England (Maine, New Hampshire, Vermont, Massachusetts, Rhode

differences in social trust even within nations. Here, too, one can make the same observations concerning the links between trust levels and social and economic indicators. Even within the continental US, social trust is correlated with household income and per capita GDP (positive), and unemployment and violent crime (negative). The granularity also allowed researchers to investigate the effect of varying trust levels on the efficiency of the market for stocks of companies incorporated in each of the ten regions.

In an efficient market, stock prices ought to respond fully and swiftly to the arrival of firm-specific news. This means, for example, that if a firm announces a positive surprise in its earnings, its stock price should rise quickly to a new equilibrium level that reflects the higher valuation. Yet, one study revealed that this rapid adjustment tended to occur only if the firm was incorporated in a high-trust region. If the firm happened to be based in a lower-trust region, investors were less likely to take the information at face-value. Their hesitation caused the initial stock price reaction to be more sluggish. In response to the news, the stock price would only partially reflect the weight of the incoming information, with the remainder of the price adjustment occurring during subsequent days and

---

Island, Connecticut), Middle Atlantic (New York, Pennsylvania, New Jersey), East North Central (Wisconsin, Michigan, Illinois, Indiana, Ohio), West North Central (Missouri, North Dakota, South Dakota, Nebraska, Kansas, Minnesota, Iowa), South Atlantic (Delaware, Maryland, Washington D.C., Virginia, West Virginia, North Carolina, South Carolina, Georgia, Florida), East South Central (Kentucky, Tennessee, Mississippi, Alabama), West South Central (Oklahoma, Texas, Arkansas, Louisiana), Rocky Mountain (Montana, Wyoming, Nevada, Utah, Colorado, Arizona, New Mexico), Northwest (Oregon, Washington, Idaho), and California.

weeks, presumably as investors sought confirming evidence. The delayed reaction, otherwise known as a post-earnings-announcement drift, or stock price momentum, was a product of investors' diminished faith in firms based in low-trust regions.[29] For the curious, the region that consistently recorded the highest trust was the Northwest (Oregon, Washington, Idaho), where average responses to the trust question were slightly above 50%; the consistently low-trust region was East South Central (Kentucky, Tennessee, Mississippi, Alabama), where averages were below 25%. It was also worthwhile to note that following the introduction of the Sarbanes-Oxley Act, a regulatory change designed to improve the reliability of corporate disclosures, the effect was eliminated. Regulation, it appears, has the possibility to raise the minimum level of trust in all firms – even in a sophisticated and well-developed capital market like in the US.

Interorganisational trust

Although scientific literature often refers to trust between firms (interorganisational trust), it is essential to remember that firms are incapable of trust. The basis for trust remains the individual (interpersonal trust). Interorganisational trust occurs when people in one organisation trust, or are favourably disposed to trusting, people in another organisation. The candidates for these interpersonal relationships are likely to be individuals whose role involves frequent external contact – for example, those involved in sales, client relationship management, purchasing, investor

---

29 Wei, C. and Zhang, L. (13 April 2016) 'Trust and Certification in Financial Markets: Evidence from Reactions to Earnings News'. Available at SSRN: ssrn.com/abstract=2469034 or dx.doi.org/10.2139/ssrn.2469034

relations, etc. Otherwise known as 'boundary spanners', these groups have the effect of institutionalising their interpersonal trust.[30] For example, the interpersonal trust between a purchasing manager and a supplier representative could lead to the establishment of cooperative norms and principles between them. Over time, as the cooperation becomes more entrenched and stable, these norms create the context wherein other interpersonal relationships between the purchasing organisation and the supplier organisation can develop.

Trust and microeconomic activity

Researchers in many countries around the world have found positive performance implications (productivity, efficiency, reduced negotiation costs, sales growth, cash flow, and return on investment) for partner firms in high-trust interorganisational relationships.[31] Reduced conflict, and smoother conflict resolution, is another benefit of inter-firm trust that is supported in the literature.[32] Firms also express greater levels of satisfaction with the business concluded with high-trust partners, which increases their willingness to do more of it. Consequently, such

---

30 Zaheer, A., McEvily, B., and Perrone, V. (1998) 'Does Trust Matter? Exploring the Effects of Interorganizational and Interpersonal Trust on Performance'. *Organization Science*, 9 (2), 141–159. doi.org/10.1287/orsc.9.2.141

31 Delbufalo, E. (2012) 'Outcomes of inter-organizational trust in supply chain relationships: a systematic literature review and a meta-analysis of the empirical evidence'. *Supply Chain Management: An International Journal*, 17 (4), 377–402.

32 Shrum, W., Chompalov, I., and Genuth, J. (2001) 'Trust, conflict and performance in scientific collaborations'. *Social Studies of Science*, 31 (5), 681–730.

firms are more certain of the continuity of their relationships, are more willing to invest, and are more likely to express future purchase intentions. Once again, interpersonal trust is the basis for interorganisational trust, but it is the interorganisational trust that produces the economic advantages.

There are several channels through which trust contributes to improved performance. Firstly, it acts as an informal governance mechanism that enhances the effectiveness of all transactions. Although formal contracts might exist, mutual trust extends to areas of the relationship that formal control mechanisms might not be able to reach, or might be less effective. Mutual trust relationships also have at their disposal social sanctions against violation, like 'shaming', that are not available to formal contracts. Improved governance thus leads to better performance through greater adherence to agreements, and readiness to conclude deals of a higher value.[33] Trust also improves business performance through its effects on operational flexibility. Business partners who can agree on arrangements with a handshake not only save time (for managers to dedicate to other, more productive endeavours), and money (on lawyers to draft contracts), but also build flexibility into those arrangements. In case of a sudden change to the operational, competitive or regulatory environment, such firms can more easily agree on new arrangements, shake hands, and get back to work. Finally, trust works through openness in the lines of communication between business partners, which allows vital information to be shared more readily and in a timely fashion. In short:

---

33 Sako, M. (1998) 'Does trust improve business performance?' in Lane, C and Backman, R. (eds.), *Trust within and between organizations: Conceptual issues and empirical applications* (pp.88–117). Oxford: Oxford University Press.

"If trust is present, people can engage in constructive interaction without pondering what hidden motives exchange partners might have, who is formally responsible for problems, or the risks of disclosing information."[34]

SUMMARY

Trust, in common parlance (and in the financial services industry), is often referred to in uncertain terms. When pushed, people see it as inescapable, but then treat it as optional. They struggle to define it, but claim to be able to recognise it when it is present. Yet trust is an essential part of our economic life. Without it, for instance, there would be no division of labour, or even the most basic form of economic organisation, like simple neighbourly cooperation. It also relates to concrete economic outcomes for countries and for firms. Decisions to invest in physical and human capital, for instance, and the establishment of credible democratic institutions, depend on the presence of trust.

Trust is also definable, which is essential if one hopes to influence its prevailing level. It is determined primarily by our impression of the other's intentions towards us. That judgement is quickly followed by a second, independent assessment about the other's ability to enact on that intention. Whenever a risky decision is to be made, that twin judgement comes into play, and determines how someone behaves. If the judgement results in a trusting

---

34 Kadefors, A. (2004) 'Trust in project relationships – inside the black box'. *International Journal of Project Management*, 22, 175–182.

state of mind, a person will exhibit trusting behaviour: an employer will hire a stranger; an investor will buy a stock; and a sponsor will entrust a manager with assets.

4 – TYPES OF TRUST

WHEN A CLIENT expresses trust in someone, it is important to be clear about what exactly it is he trusts, especially if a service provider wants to influence it. We saw in the previous chapter that investors can express trust in the reliability of a firm's corporate announcements as a function solely of where that firm is incorporated. Does the client trust someone as a function of his postcode? We have discussed the concept of 'institutionalised' trust. Does the client trust someone because he works at a particular firm? We have also illustrated the trust that exists between an individual purchasing manager and supplier representative. Does this mean that the client trusts someone because of familiarity with that person? The answer to all these questions is: yes.

Trust can develop as a product of personal contact, but it can also be 'attributed' to someone by virtue of the role that person fulfils, or because of the rules and regulations that apply to that role. By looking at trust relationships with varying degrees of resolution, one distinguishes three types of trust: system trust, role trust and interpersonal trust. In this chapter, we will illustrate the different kinds of trust relationship that can exist using the example of a firefighter, a commonly trusted counterparty. We will also show how the three trust types manifest themselves in the financial services industry. In each case, the means to influencing the degree of trust is different.

SYSTEM TRUST

People frequently express a high degree of trust in firefighters. They do this even though many of them have neither met a firefighter, nor had any reason to call on any firefighting services. What is it exactly that they trust? Part of this trust comes from the confidence they have in emergency services in general. These services have been designed so that anyone requiring emergency help need only dial a dedicated telephone number to connect to emergency specialists on permanent standby. So people trust that if their house should catch fire, a simple call to the emergency number will result in a connection to the fire services, and that firefighters will be immediately dispatched to their location. Confidence in emergency specialists, therefore, is partly a product of the confidence people have in the reliability and predictability of the system of alert and response. System trust exists when the operating context or environment has variables and relationships that are reliable and predictable. The public trusts the system in which firefighters operate.

System trust in the financial services industry

A demonstration of system trust in the financial markets can be seen in investors' reaction to economic news. Investors are swift to buy and sell securities following the announcement of economic data because they are confident that the system provides accurate data concerning employment, inflation, growth, etc. If they have doubts about the accuracy of the data, the response will not be so swift, because investors will tend to wait for confirming data before placing their orders. The same applies to firm-specific data, like revenues and earnings, disposals and acquisitions, appointments and board meetings. Investors need to have confidence in the reliability of corporate disclosures before reacting to them. This is why, prior to the introduction of the Sarbanes-Oxley Act, investors responded sluggishly to announcements from firms incorporated in certain regions of the US.[35] The mistrust was not directed at any individual firm; all firms lacked some system trust because regulations in those regions concerning corporate disclosures were perceived as being less stringent. Even firms that adhered to higher standards than those required by local laws – i.e. were objectively more trustworthy – would have been attributed lower trust evaluations because they operated in a system that was perceived as less reliable. The introduction of the Act raised the level of system trust. All firms in the region could benefit from improved trust, including those whose standards were already high and, therefore, had no changes to make.

Across most of the rich world, the rule of law, strict financial regulation and strong democratic institutions mean that consumers express a high level of system trust in financial service providers. Despite the occasional corporate scandal

---

35 Wei, C. and Zhang, L., (30 October 2014) 'Trust and Market Efficiency'. Available at SSRN: ssrn.com/abstract=2517142 or dx.doi.org/10.2139/ssrn.2517142

(Bernie Madoff, Enron, etc.), system trust in these jurisdictions remains relatively robust. So, when investors hand money over to an asset manager, they might be anxious about the riskiness of the securities the manager might invest in, but they do not worry excessively about the manager stealing the money, or the government confiscating it. Indeed, without system trust nobody would invest in stocks, open bank accounts, seek credit, or participate in financial markets. All regulated financial institutions, therefore, earn some of their clients' trust simply because they operate in a system the client trusts. In parts of the developing world, in contrast, property rights are less reliable, and there might be few strong institutions to defend them. Service providers in these jurisdictions benefit from little or no system trust – even the ones that adhere to high standards of governance.

Regulatory bodies, rating agencies, certification organisations, and the judiciary, all play a role in supporting system trust. The institution that plays the central role, however, is the government, as this is the body that designs the system. One would imagine, therefore, that a trusted government would be good news for financial services providers and their clients. Sadly, though, trust among individuals is not the same as trust in governments and in political institutions.[36] The World Values Survey data reveals that individuals who express an elevated level of trust in their fellow countrymen are significantly more likely to buy stocks and other risky assets and, when they do, to invest a larger share of their wealth in them. And trust among individuals has been

---

36 Guiso, L., Sapienza, P., and Zingales, L. (2008) 'Trusting the stock market'. *The Journal of Finance*, 63 (6), 2557–2600. dx.doi.org/10.1111/j.1540-6261.2008.01408.x

rising in many countries in recent years (typically those in which it was already high). At the same time, though, the Organisation for Economic Co-operation and Development (OECD) has tracked a deterioration in public trust in the governments of its member countries since the 2007/08 global financial crisis. It even saw it necessary to publish guidelines to help governments improve it.[37] Not surprisingly, its publication drew attention to the need for political integrity and action against corruption. The OECD also recognised that system trust requires that governments be reliable (managing public budgets, anticipating and dealing with crises, etc.), and predictable (transparency of policy design, decision-making with stakeholder consultation, policies fully implemented and fairly enforced).

Individual firms, like individual firefighters, have little influence over the level of trust in the system in which they operate. Furthermore, firms do not 'earn' system trust; they get it by default if they are part of a trusted system. All they can decide is whether they want to be, or are able to be, part of that system. For a firm to improve its system trust, therefore, it must move from a system where trust is low, to one in which trust is higher. An unregulated firm could submit to the oversight of a respected regulator or auditor; a company incorporated in a low-trust region could move its base to a high-trust region; or a firm in a developing country could seek to establish itself in a developed country. These steps probably involve costs, but are necessary to win system trust, and to be able to compete with firms that already enjoy it.

---

37 OECD. (2017) *Trust and Public Policy: How Better Governance Can Help Rebuild Public Trust*, OECD Publishing, Paris. dx.doi.org/10.1787/9789264268920-en

ROLE TRUST

So, you have called the emergency services to attend to your burning house. The firefighters have arrived. Although you might never have met any of them before, you trust them. Why? Because they are firefighters. The public is confident that the men and women employed to do this job have the training and equipment necessary to extinguish the fire. People have trust in the 'role' of firefighters. Role trust exists when the entrusted counterparty is believed to possess the necessary expertise to do the job.[38] For the public to express role trust, people must have some knowledge about the skills and competence of the counterparty, in some cases even without having had any direct experience. Role trust, therefore, involves due diligence. It relies on information such as reputation, brand, references, certification, diplomas and any other tangible information that signals what performance is to be expected from a potential exchange partner.

Role trust and the financial services industry

Asset managers and financial advisors differ from firefighters in one important respect: whereas the training and certification of the latter can reasonably be expected to correlate with success on the job, the same cannot be said for the former. Diplomas and certificates are no assurance of a 'star' asset manager, but sponsors try to infer from them nonetheless.

---

38 Also referred to as cognitive or calculative trust.

Selectors rightly want to hire asset managers who are intelligent (educational attainment being the most frequently used proxy for intelligence). Indeed, whatever the enterprise, the likelihood of its success will be greater in the hands of intelligent individuals.[39] Yet, the positive relationship between intelligence and investment performance is weak.

For instance, potential asset managers are often required to hold postgraduate degrees – MBAs or PhDs – though generally neither of these educational attainments predict better investment performance. The exceptions are for asset managers who graduated from a business school where average GMAT scores are high, who attended a *Businessweek* Top 30 MBA School, or who are hired by a firm that employs many asset managers with PhDs. This small subset of individuals does perform better.[40,41] The researchers concede, though, that this finding might not be solely due to their cognitive ability, or even to the environment of greater scientific rigour that might prevail in firms where PhDs are abundant; these managers might simply be exploiting the better social and professional connections that they (and their colleagues) established at more prestigious schools. Similarly, the CFA professional qualification only appears to be associated with better investment performance

39 Strenze, T. (2015) 'Intelligence and Success'. In *Handbook of Intelligence: Evolutionary Theory, Historical Perspective, and Current Concepts*. Goldstein, S. et al. (eds.), dx.doi.org/10.1007/978-1-4939-1562-0-25, © Springer Science+Business Media New York 2015.

40 Gottesman, A. and Morey, M. (2006) 'Manager Education and Mutual Fund Performance'. *Journal of Empirical Finance*, 13 (1), 145–182.

41 Busse, J. A., Goyal, A. and Wahal, S. (2010) 'Performance and Persistence in Institutional Investment Management'. *The Journal of Finance*, 65 (2), 765–790.

while the candidates are studying for the examinations. The authors of a study of sell-side research analysts observed that performance improved as candidates went through the CFA Program, but such improvements stopped after completion.[42]

Once again, the goal of this book is not to judge the accuracy or reliability of the signals sponsors use to make their selection decisions, only to identify them and the role they play. The educational-attainment signal clearly is not reliable, but it is still one of the elements to which clients are attentive when they attribute role trust. To improve role trust, therefore, financial service providers have an obvious interest in strengthening the number and quality of the signals clients refer to during their due diligence processes. This means securing certifications and qualifications, enhancing brands and reputations, and delivering on public promises. Some role trust accrues solely because of the firm for which a person works.[43] So, for individual asset managers and financial advisors, this might also mean moving from a firm whose reputation or brand is weak, to one whose repute will endow them with greater role trust.

---

42 Kang, Q., Li, X. and Su, T. (2012) 'CFA Certification Program and Sell-Side Analysts'. Available at SSRN: ssrn.com/abstract=2137312 or dx.doi.org/10.2139/ssrn.2137312

43 Swan, J. E., Bowers, M. R., Richardson, L. D. (1999) 'Customer Trust in the Salesperson: An Integrative Review and Meta-Analysis of the Empirical Literature'. *Journal of Business Research*, 44, (2), 93–107.

INTERPERSONAL TRUST

One of the firefighters, a tall, bearded fellow, with ridiculously large hands, instructs his colleague to escort your bewildered neighbours away from the scene. He looks down at you and asks if you were the one who raised the alarm. He says his name is Alex, and recommends that you get yourself checked out by one of the medics. Smoke inhalation, he says, can sometimes have delayed effects on the lungs. You already trust firefighters, but this isn't just any firefighter; this is Alex. Alex wants to know who you are and what you have done. Alex is concerned for your immediate well-being, and for your long-term health. You trust Alex even more than you trust all the other members of his crew.

Interpersonal trust exists when the entrusted counterparty is motivated to act in the other's interests, and is capable of doing so. This is the kind of trust that one individual has toward another specific individual. Unlike in the World Values Survey, or in a Trust Game, where the people being evaluated are anonymous, interpersonal trust requires some familiarity with the counterparty. The trustor's perceptions of the trustee's intentions figure large in the emergence of interpersonal trust; perceptions of the other's abilities come a distant second. Even if the house were to burn to the ground, you would still trust Alex the firefighter because he cares about you.

Interpersonal trust in the financial services industry

Empirical data on the trust relationships between fund sponsors and asset managers, and the consequences thereof, is very sparse. However, there have been several studies concerning the relationship between financial advisors and their retail clients. Clearly, the financial risks involved for retail clients are not identical in nature, and certainly not in magnitude, to those of institutional investors. The signals they attend to when they evaluate their service providers are also likely to differ. Yet, they do share some vulnerabilities – for instance, the information asymmetry – especially at the outset of the relationship. Retail investors also face the problem of not being able to accurately evaluate the quality of the service until long after they have acquired it. When it comes to the goal of their evaluations, and the consequences of a favourable judgement, the research shows that retail and institutional investors are very similar.

Evidence from a survey of clients of a UK-based financial advisory firm suggests that, for retail clients too, trust can be conceptualised as two-dimensional.[44] Clients looked for indications that their advisors were motivated to act in their interests. Emotionally, they wanted to feel secure and cared for. Clients also sought indications that advisors were competent, reliable and predictable. They, too, wanted to have confidence in their service provider's ability to deliver on his promises. A high level of trust, meaning a lofty evaluation on both these dimensions, increased economic outcomes for financial advisors.

---

44 Johnson, D. and Grayson, K. (2005) 'Cognitive and affective trust in service relationships'. *Journal of Business Research*, 58 (4), 500–507.

Not only did it improve sales effectiveness – i.e. the salesperson's success in achieving his desired sales outcomes – it contributed significantly to clients' satisfaction and willingness to meet the advisor in the future. An earlier meta-study also concluded that positive interactions between a customer and a salesperson rise modestly with increasing levels of trust.[45] The same study also summarised evidence of a salesperson's modest influence on the level of trust held by the client.

A further study, again from the retail financial services industry, revealed that the salesperson's 'likeability' was not a factor in the emergence of trust. Clients didn't trust the salesperson just because they liked him; the drivers of trust were the salesperson's customer-orientation and intention, as well as the salesperson's expertise. The likeability score only influenced the client's willingness to recommend the salesperson to others. Thus, concluded the authors, likeability may only be helpful for acquiring new customers, not for developing long-lasting trust relationships with existing clients. In the financial services industry, being liked might be a prerequisite to play, but it is not sufficient to win.[46]

---

45 Swan, J. E., Bowers, M. R. and Richardson, L. D. (1999) 'Customer Trust in the Salesperson: An Integrative Review and Meta-Analysis of the Empirical Literature'. *Journal of Business Research*, 44 (2), 93–107.

46 Guenzi, P. and Georges, L. (2010) 'Interpersonal trust in commercial relationships: antecedents and consequences of customer trust in the salesperson'. *European Journal of Marketing*, 44, 114–138.

Interpersonal trust is a two-way street

Interpersonal trust does not depend solely on the trustee's characteristics – or, rather, how the trustor perceives those characteristics. The trustor's own traits also play a part. Similarly, the relative status of the trustor and trustee, and the context in which their interaction takes place, will also influence the emergence of interpersonal trust.

The trustor-specific factors relate to the individual's underlying propensity to trust other people in general. Some people are naturally more willing to embark on new relationships without first gathering exhaustive information about the unknown other. This propensity to trust is a mostly stable dispositional trait, which depends on factors like one's personality, life experiences or cultural background. It is related to the trait 'optimism' – glass half-full vs half-empty – yet distinct from it. A high propensity to trust is really a willingness to be vulnerable to another.[47] Organisations hoping to encourage interorganisational trust with partner firms have an interest to place such individuals in 'boundary spanning' roles, such as purchasing, sales and client relations.

The relative status of the trustee and trustor is also important to the emergence of interpersonal trust. Is the relationship equal-status, for example, or superior-subordinate? Research has found that high-status individuals (perhaps because they assume that subordinates will trust leaders anyway) tend to perceive others

---

47 Frazier, M. L., Johnson, P. D. and Fainshmidt, S. (2013) 'Development and validation of a propensity to trust scale'. *Journal of Trust Research*, 3 (2), 76–97.

as more benevolent and, therefore, more trustworthy.[48] However, the contrary might be the case in the opposite direction. Hence, trust is encouraged when both exchange partners perceive the other as having the same status as themselves.

Contextual factors in interpersonal trust refer primarily to the social networks in which people operate. For example, if a trustor and a trustee share a trusted network connection, a mutual friend, interpersonal trust tends to be higher, especially if that third-party is a high-status individual. If a trustee shares a demographic resemblance with many others in the social network, this also tends to promote interpersonal trust. In an organisational setting, incentives or reward structures influence the emergence of interpersonal trust. If rewards encourage cooperative behaviour and value team effort, rather than competitive behaviour and individual effort, trust levels tend to be higher.[49]

---

48 Lount Jr., R. B. and Pettit, N. C. (2012) 'The social context of trust: The role of status'. *Organizational Behavior and Human Decision Processes*, 117 (1), 15–23.

49 Hill, N. S., et al. (2009) 'Organizational context and face-to-face interaction: Influences on the development of trust and collaborative behaviors in computer-mediated groups'. *Organizational Behavior and Human Decision Processes*, 108 (2), 187–201.

THE INTERACTION BETWEEN THE THREE TYPES OF TRUST

System trust, role trust and interpersonal trust are nested together. Although it appears that system trust supports role trust, which in turn facilitates interpersonal trust, the causality is in both directions. There would not be any delegated asset management industry, for instance, unless someone had first trusted someone else with his money. This suggests that interpersonal trust came first. Yet, without the possibility of some form of sanction, if not legal then at least social, against nascent asset managers who renege on their agreements, it is questionable whether even this early mandate would have materialised. Interpersonal trust is, in any case, the more fundamental and the more robust of the three.

Imagine a situation where public trust in the system is shaken, or breaks down. An example was seen during the 2009 outbreak of the deadly influenza strain, H1N1, otherwise known as 'swine flu'. The pandemic, and the public's reaction to it, provided data for several research studies into the impact of public trust in global health organisations, government ministries and the media ('the system'), and what happens when this trust is eroded. Two studies in Italy revealed that people who expressed trust in the health ministry, and in the media, were more likely to adopt the recommended preventative behaviours – even if they thought the media had exaggerated the risk, and that the ministry was doing a poor job in handling the pandemic. Counterparties who had built up a reserve of trust with the public prior to the pandemic were able to draw upon it as system trust faltered. This was the key to understanding the public's compliance.[50] Over the course of the pandemic, the public's trust in the system declined. A second study revealed that in situations where the recommendations issued by government agencies differed from those issued by general practitioners and paediatricians, people followed the advice of their physicians. Even as system trust crumbled, role trust and interpersonal trust remained intact.[51]

In the case of the financial services industry, one only needs to think back to the 2007/08 financial crisis to see an example of faltering system trust. Asset prices collapsed, there were bank failures, queues in front of some high-street moneylenders, and government bailouts. Many people feared they would not be able to get their money out of the bank. For some, this fear proved to be justified. Trust in the system suffered a blow. However, amidst this declining system trust, some firms negotiated the crisis quite well. Stakeholders in these firms effectively said: 'I have little faith in the rules and regulations to defend my interests, but I still trust the firm that is managing my money to do everything in its power to protect my assets.' Role trust remained intact. Now imagine that events revealed that the management of the trusted firm had failed in their oversight of some key operations. Stakeholders might lose

---

50 Prati, G., Pietrantoni, L. and Zani, B. (2011) 'Compliance with recommendations for pandemic influenza H1N1 2009: The role of trust and personal beliefs'. *Health Education Research*, 26, 761–769.

51 Ferrante, G., Baldissera, S., Moghadam, P. F., Carrozzi, G., Trinito, M. O. and Salmaso, S. (2011) 'Surveillance of perceptions, knowledge, attitudes and behaviors of the Italian adult population (18–69 years) during the 2009–2010 A/H1N1 influenza pandemic'. *European Journal of Epidemiology*, 26, 211–219.

role trust. They might no longer believe the firm's employees have the skills to perform the necessary tasks. Despite this, they might still trust Mary, the portfolio manager who had managed the account for years, to act competently even though some of her colleagues appear not to be up to the task. Interpersonal trust can survive even when role trust and system trust have been compromised.

SUMMARY

One must make a distinction between three types of trust: system trust, role trust and interpersonal trust. Individual firms do not earn system trust; they are credited with it by default depending on the institutions, laws, and regulations that govern the jurisdiction in which they choose to operate. They need only to choose the 'right' jurisdiction, regulator, auditor, etc., to acquire it in the eyes of their clients. Role trust is credited to the entire class of individuals who fulfil a specific role. It must be 'earned' only in the sense that one must first qualify to be part of the trusted class, e.g. one must become a firefighter, be awarded a doctoral degree, or be employed by a well-reputed firm. Due diligence by sponsors is sensitive to the signals that identify an individual as a member of a class, even though class membership is not necessarily a reliable indicator of future performance. Interpersonal trust relies on familiarity with an individual or group. This kind of trust must be earned by those individuals. Critically, it depends on the trustor's perception of the trustee's intentions and, to a lesser degree, of their abilities. It is also influenced by the trustor's personality traits, the relative status of the exchange partners, and the context in which the exchange takes place. The three types of trust are closely interlinked, but interpersonal trust is the more robust. As it is also the one that service providers can actively influence, it will be explored in greater detail in the next chapter.

5 — WARMTH AND COMPETENCE

"Is your financial advisor any good?"

"He's OK, I guess."

I N THE CONVERSATION above, two protagonists discuss a financial advisor. Although it is a familiar way to ask for an opinion, and a common way to give one, neither the question, nor the response, reflect the complexity of the judgements that underlie it. This is because we do not judge others along a good-versus-bad scale. Indeed, our evaluation of others is not even one-dimensional; it has two dimensions. One is qualitative, and is an attempt to assess the person's motivation and future intentions. The second is quantitative, and concerns the proven past ability of the person. There is also evidence to suggest that intentions play a more important role in these evaluations than abilities. The combination of judgements along these two dimensions is a global impression of the individual which, when risk is involved, is what we refer to as interpersonal trust. Service providers who are trusted are likely to have more satisfied clients, to have more positive interactions, and do higher-value business with them. If those individuals involved in high-trust interpersonal relationships can 'institutionalise' them, i.e. set similar norms for cooperation and communication in their respective firms, interorganisational trust can bring additional economic advantages.

The missing 'it' is seemingly found in these high-trust relationships. Therefore, this chapter will focus on these two dimensions, and look at how they shape our impressions of other people. We will also show how these impressions elicit emotions and fuel behaviours in systematic and predictable ways.

DUAL DIMENSIONS OF IMPRESSION FORMATION

Although what constitutes, or signals, 'warmth' and 'competence' might vary around the world,[52] the evaluation nonetheless takes place along these two dimensions.[53]

'Warmth' refers to a benevolent orientation that puts others before self. This judgement is about whether others are:

• kind

---

52 Cuddy, A. J. C., Fiske, S. T. and Glick, P. (2008) 'Warmth and Competence As Universal Dimensions of Social Perception: The Stereotype Content Model and the BIAS Map'. *Advances in Experimental Social Psychology*, 40, 61–149.

53 Cuddy, A. J. C., Fiske, S. T., Kwan, V. S. Y., Glick, P., Demoulin, S., Leyens, J. P., et al. (2009) 'Stereotype content model across cultures: towards universal similarities and some differences'. *British Journal of Social Psychology*, 48, 1–33.

- friendly

- honest

- moral

- accommodating

- helpful

- tolerant

- fair

- generous

- understanding.

The term 'competence' refers to the ability to make desired outcomes happen. This judgement is about the other's:

- relative strength (or weakness)

- power

- efficacy

- status

- resources

- skills

- knowledge

- intelligence

- confidence

- creativity.

Both judgements can be readily associated with the preferences expressed by plan sponsors and investment consultants in their selection process. Non-performance factors regroup elements consistent with warmth judgements. They focus on the managers' intentions towards the client and their motivation to put other's interests ahead of their own. Performance factors, and other demonstrations of the asset manager's past ability, are competence judgements. They reflect managers' ability to make desired outcomes happen, namely, to deliver superior investment performance. Of the two dimensions, research has consistently shown that warmth is primary. It is the first judgement to be made,[54] it is made faster,[55] and it carries the most weight in the evaluation. Knowing whether the intentions of the other are good or bad is more important than knowing what the other can do.[56]

The response, *"OK"*, to the opening question, *"Is your financial advisor any good?"*, is one-dimensional. On a good–bad scale, it implies something in the middle. However, if one considers the two dimensions the client is *actually* using (possibly without even being aware of it), it becomes clear that the advisor is failing on at least one of them. If the client is pushed for a more discriminating response, one might uncover one of the following:

> *"He is very knowledgeable and creative, but I don't believe he understands my needs, or is working primarily to maximise my outcomes."*

54 Abele, A. E. and Bruckmüller, S. (2011) 'The Bigger one of the "Big Two"? Preferential processing of communal information'. *Journal of Experimental Social Psychology* 47, 935–948. doi: 10.1016/j.jesp.2011.03.028.

55 Ybarra, O., Chan, E., and Park, D. (2001) 'Young and old adults' concerns about morality and competence'. *Motivation and Emotion*, 25, 85–100.

56 Earle, T. C. (2010) 'Trust in Risk Management: A Model-Based Review of Empirical Research', *Risk Analysis*, 30 (4), 541–574. doi: 10.1111/j.1539-6924.2010.01398.x

"He works tirelessly to find products that match my needs, and he always has time for me, but he often seems overwhelmed, and out of his depth."

THE EVOLUTIONARY ORIGINS OF WARMTH AND COMPETENCE

Researchers attribute the ubiquity of warmth and competence judgements to our evolutionary origins. In early human societies, it would have been necessary to instantly assess strangers in order to formulate an initial response. The first judgement that early man would have had to make is whether this unknown other is a friend or a foe, one of 'us' or one of 'them', a giver or a taker. This judgement is about whether the stranger has friendly or unfriendly intentions towards us. This is always the judgement that is made first, because it determines our approach-avoidance response. Thereafter, a judgement is made about the other's competence, in other words, the ability to act on his or its intentions. At its most basic, this question is: can I eat it, or can it eat me? If the stranger is judged to be hostile and powerful, i.e. wants to take and can take, then flight is the obvious response. A powerless hostile, who wants to take, but cannot, would be better crushed underfoot. Neither of these responses is appropriate for those we judge as having benevolent intentions towards us. A powerful friend, one who wants to give, and can give, would make an excellent companion. Even a powerless friend, one who wants to give, but cannot, might prove to be a useful accessory one day.

The way people categorise animals reflects the visceral nature of these judgements. These are our gut reactions, like those of our evolutionary ancestors. One study asked participants to rate 25 common animals on a nine-point scale in a variety of categories.[57] Some of these categories reflected warmth (warm, well-intentioned, friendly), and some competence (competent, skilful, intelligent). The results of the survey were averaged across each dimension, and so could also be displayed on a four-quadrant graphic.

FIGURE 5.1 – WARMTH AND COMPETENCE IN ANIMALS

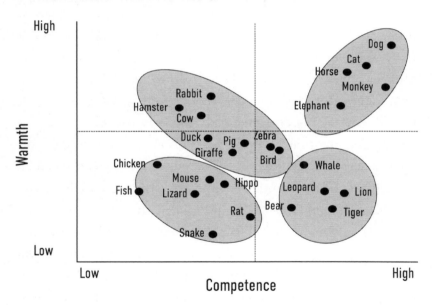

Source: Adapted from Sevillano, V. and Fiske, S. T. (2016).

---

57 Sevillano, V. and Fiske, S. T. (2016) 'Warmth and competence in animals'. *Journal of Applied Social Psychology*, 46, 276–293.

A cluster analysis of the results (illustrated by the dark circles) revealed four notable groupings. The researchers labelled them 'predators' (low-warmth/high-competence); 'companions' (high-warmth/high-competence); 'prey' (high-warmth/low-competence); and 'pests' (low-warmth/low-competence). Here, too, the universally 'good' (dog, cat or horse) are easy to identify, as are the universally 'bad' (snake, rat and lizard). But many perceptions were ambivalent, like cow and zebra, and strikingly different, like hamster and tiger.

STEREOTYPES, EMOTIONS, AND BEHAVIOUR

Whatever judgements one person might make about another, it is important to remember that these are only perceptions, not the genuine traits of that person. For example, an elephant's intentions towards a human might not be more benevolent than those of a hippo. A horse might not be more intelligent or capable than a bear. Yet, we *perceive* them as having these traits; they are stereotypes. These stereotypical characterisations are a product of the limited experience we have had with these creatures, for example, in zoos, farms, and television wildlife programmes. These perceptions are nonetheless important because they elicit specific emotions, and those emotions give rise to specific behaviours.[58]

---

58 Cuddy, A. J. C., Fiske, S. T. and Glick, P. (2007) 'The BIAS Map: Behaviors from intergroup affect and stereotypes'. *Journal of Personality and Social Psychology*, 92, 631–648.

FIGURE 5.2 – EMOTIONS EVOKED BY WARMTH–COMPETENCE STEREOTYPES

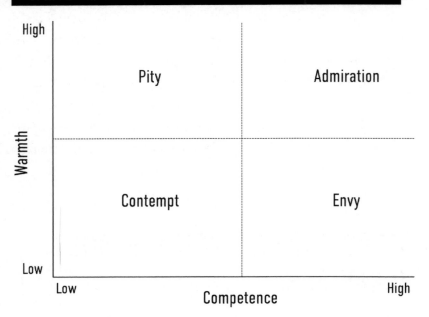

Source: Adapted from Cuddy, Fiske and Glick (2007).

Warm and competent

The emotion evoked when we perceive someone as high-warmth and high-competence is admiration. These are the 'lovable stars',[59] the kind of people we adore, respect, imitate, are proud of, and want to follow. Sometimes this perception arises because the person embodies a cultural default or a social ideal, for example, a celebrity. In most cases, however, the perception is purely self-serving. As we tend to see ourselves in these flattering terms, we will tend to perceive anyone who resembles us in the same terms.

---

59 Casciaro, T. and Sousa Lobo, M. (2005) 'Competent jerks, lovable fools, and the formation of social networks'. *Harvard Business Review*, 83, 92–99.

> Admiration = You are the same as me. I am friendly and successful, so you must be too.

Competent but cold

When we perceive someone as competent, but cold, the emotion elicited is typically one of envy. These people are not like us, but (annoyingly) are nonetheless successful. Due to their perceived competence, we begrudgingly tolerate and associate with these people, and do what they recommend. Their perceived ability to use their competence to harm us might also make us feel compelled to accommodate them. This is the best case. Yet we do not genuinely believe they have our best interests at heart, even though we might not have any proof that this is the case. Should any proof emerge, and they become colder in our perception, our subdued hostility towards this group would resurface and, in the worst case, we would revolt against them.

> Envy = You are not like me, but you are successful anyway.

Warm but incompetent

Pity is the emotion most commonly aroused when we perceive others as warm but incompetent. We recognise that such people *mean well*. The problem is that we also recognise that they lack the skills, resources, knowledge, etc. to follow through on these intentions. In the best case, we will support and defend these people because we believe they would do the same for us. In the worst case, however, we will ignore or neglect them because we cannot see what useful purpose they serve.

Pity = You are friendly, but powerless.

Cold and incompetent

Finally, the emotion reserved for those we perceive as cold and incompetent is contempt, or even disgust. We not only consider this group to be hostile, but our perception of their powerlessness might encourage us to think that simple avoidance does not go far enough; we might want to eliminate them completely.

Contempt = You are hostile and powerless.

Emotions are difficult to suppress

Out of a desire not to appear uncharitable, or even outright nasty, study participants might be reluctant to report the full range of emotions they experience when considering people in each of these various groups. In other words, the bottom, left-hand quadrant might not be as full as it might otherwise be. However, their faces invariably give away their true sentiments. In one set of experiments, scientists measured the activity in the smile muscles of participants' faces as they were exposed to images of mundane events happening to people categorised in each of the four quadrants.[60] Some of those events were good (like getting indoors just before it pours with rain, or discovering a free concert in the park), and some were bad (like getting splashed by a taxi, or accidentally walking into a glass door).

---

60 Cikara, M., Fiske, S. T. (2012) 'Stereotypes and Schadenfreude: Behavioral and physiological markers of pleasure at others' misfortunes'. *Social Psychological and Personality Science*, 3 (1), 63–71.

Not surprisingly, people tended to smile when good things happened to high-warmth individuals, whether they were judged competent or not. Even when contemplating people in the 'pity' group, respondents showed a greater tendency to smile when good things happened to them than when bad things happened. The 'envy' group was unique in provoking more smiles when bad things happened than good.

Emotions provoke behaviours

In terms of the behavioural responses to these emotions, the primary dimension – warmth – invariably decides the 'best case' and the 'worst case'. The other person's intentions towards us are so essential in our social judgements, it always provokes an active response. When we perceive others as having benevolent intentions, we are motivated to help them, actively. This is the 'best case', and it is known as **active facilitation**. In contrast, we reserve our most hostile responses, the 'worst case', for those we perceive as having malevolent intentions towards us. We are motivated to oppose this group, and will do so actively. This behaviour is known as **active harm**.

FIGURE 5.3 – BEHAVIOURS PROVOKED BY WARMTH–COMPETENCE STEREOTYPES

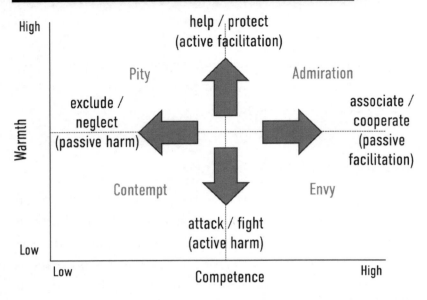

Source: Adapted from Cuddy, Fiske, and Glick (2007).

The secondary dimension – competence – being only a judgement of others' ability to act on their intentions, provokes passive behaviours. We might not be the authors of the benefit or the injury that befalls this group, for instance, but it will have our tacit approval. We will allow ourselves to be co-opted by high-competence groups, or feel obliged to go along with them. This type of behaviour is known as **passive facilitation**. Similarly, we ignore or neglect low-competence groups, a behaviour known as **passive harm**.

WARMTH AND COMPETENCE IN SOCIAL PERCEPTIONS

The twin judgements of warmth and competence explain a substantial part of our overall impressions of other individuals and groups.[61] Once again, it is the warmth judgement that predicts those impressions the most strongly – cold people always leave negative overall impressions, and vice versa.[62] Furthermore, these impressions are not limited to human beings. We have already seen, for example, that people can make warmth-competence judgements about animals. Researchers have also discovered that consumers make the same judgements about corporate brands, and have shown that they predict the same emotions and behaviours, through brand loyalty and purchase intentions.[63] Our focus here, though, is on global impressions of other individuals – namely, clients' impressions of their financial service providers. We will therefore look more closely at some common social perceptions to show where financial service providers fit.

---

61 Some authors (e.g. Wojciszke, B., Bazinska, R. and Jaworski, M. (1998)) have estimated that warmth-competence judgements explain in excess of 80% of the variance of our global impression of unknown others.

62 Wojciszke, B., Bazinska, R. and Jaworski, M. (1998) 'On the dominance of moral categories in impression formation'. *Personality and Social Psychology Bulletin*, 24, 1245–1257.

63 Kervyn, N., Fiske, S. T., and Malone, C. (2012) 'Brands as Intentional Agents Framework: How Perceived Intentions and Ability Can Map Brand Perception'. *Journal of Consumer Psychology: The Official Journal of the Society for Consumer Psychology*, 22, 1–20.

Warmth-competence stereotypes: social groups in the US

As warmth-competence judgements are merely perceptions, they are not necessarily accurate. In the first instance, they might only reflect popular stereotypes. Later, through repeated encounters with the individual or group, these perceptions are prone to be refined or revised. Hence, judgements, emotions and behaviours can and do change over time. The evidence that we will present concerning warmth-competence judgements, therefore, can only represent snapshots of these assessments at a given place and time. Nonetheless, some of these stereotypes do seem to be particularly tenacious.

One study of social groups in the US revealed an enduring feature of those considered to be high-warmth and high-competence: they tend to resemble those asked to make the judgements.[64] There is an egocentric bias to our perceptions of others. As we see ourselves as kind and generous, intelligent and successful, we tend to attribute these traits to people who are like us. Hence, when the average judgements are mapped to a four-quadrant graphic, Americans tend to place 'Americans' in the top right-hand quadrant. The 'middle class' and 'Christians' are classed as high-warmth, high-competence for the same reasons. This cluster also tends to include cultural defaults, like 'housewives', who are particularly revered, even by those who are not housewives.

---

64 This applies to individualist cultures, like the US and Western Europe. Collectivist cultures, like in East Asia, tend not to display this in-group favouritism.

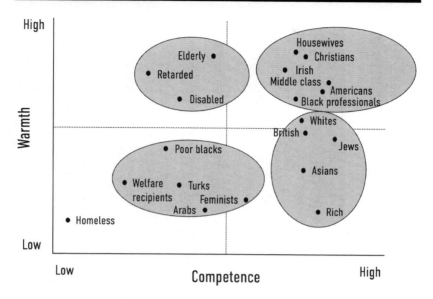

FIGURE 5.4 – WARMTH–COMPETENCE STEREOTYPES: SOCIAL GROUPS IN THE US

Source: Adapted from Cuddy, Fiske, and Glick (2007).

The low-warmth, high-competence cluster included a social group that maps to this quadrant in the US and in every country where the question is asked: the rich. Those described as 'rich' cannot resemble the majority. They are not 'one of us', and are thus suspected of harbouring malevolent intent. At the same time, their wealth signals success, and so implies competence. The same reasoning puts 'Asians', 'Jews' and the 'British' in the bottom right-hand corner. Many Americans perceive these groups to be sufficiently distant and aloof to warrant suspicion, but economically successful enough to fuel jealousy.

The 'elderly' and 'disabled' appear in the high-warmth, low-competence quadrant of the graphic. Respondents probably found it easier to imagine themselves among the former than the latter, which might explain why they rate the elderly as warmer than the disabled. Such perceptions also have implications for the degree of active help and support wider society offers to these respective groups.

Finally, in the lower left-hand quadrant, respondents placed those they perceive as low-warmth and low-competence. These groups are also perceived as distant and dissimilar, like 'immigrants', but also as economically unsuccessful, like 'welfare recipients'. One would predict that wider society would shun these groups. In the worst case, for those perceived as particularly cold, avoidance would not be enough; those groups might be subject to active harm because they are believed to be freeloaders. It is noteworthy that the group labelled 'homeless' was rated so poorly on both dimensions that it defied all attempts to cluster. This research, at least, revealed it to be the most contemptible group in US society.

Warmth-competence stereotypes: the European Union

A cross-cultural study in the European Union (EU) elicited warmth-competence judgements from people in several member states about their own citizens, and about citizens of the other states. Predictably, the results reflected some popular cultural stereotypes – for instance, a contrast between northern and southern Europeans. Overall, Europeans delivered similar impressions of themselves as others delivered to them, and most impressions were ambivalent. There was one notable exception, though. While no member state rated another in the high-warmth, high-competence quadrant, this is precisely where the French rated themselves.

FIGURE 5.5 – WARMTH-COMPETENCE STEREOTYPES: THE EUROPEAN UNION

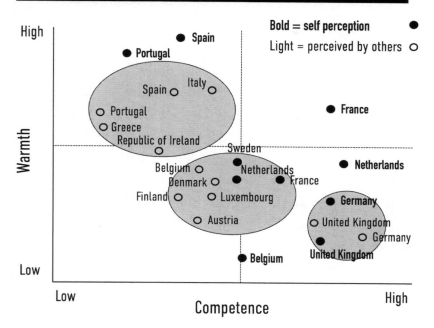

Source: Adapted from Cuddy et al. (2009).

These perceptions, gathered just ahead of the 2007/08 financial crisis could have proved useful in predicting how EU citizens would view the consequences of the crisis, and whether they would endorse the financial support extended to the hardest-hit countries: sympathy (pity) or schadenfreude (envy); tough love (admiration) or tough luck (contempt). They are also informative for understanding how EU nations react to the news that one of their members wants to leave the club.

Detour: Brexit

Brexit – the departure of the United Kingdom from the EU – is probably the clearest expression of low warmth. Brexit signifies to other EU states that UK citizens prefer to be part of the 'out-group' rather than the 'in-group', that they put their own interests ahead of those of the Union. What could be colder than asking for a divorce? As warmth is the primary dimension of social perception, it provokes active behaviours, active harm in this case. Therefore, one would expect EU populations to want to exact some punishment on the UK. The 'good news', however, is that, according to data from the 2007 study, the UK was not perceived as warm before the Brexit decision – only Germans were rated by others as colder. This means the shift in perception on this dimension, if any at all, is very modest. All that happened was that covert hostility towards the UK became overt. Compare this to the situation that might have prevailed had Italy or Spain elected to quit the EU. The dramatic shift in perceptions, in this case from very warm to cold, would have provoked extremely hostile reactions from the other member states.

Brexit's impact on EU perceptions of the UK's competence is less obvious. Some people might consider the UK electorate's decision to be shrewd, while others to be foolhardy. Assuming opinions are unchanged since 2007, the UK is still perceived to be a high-competence nation. The EU's desire to attach itself to a successful economic model (envy), and the fear that the UK might use its competence (influence, resources, connections) to the EU's detriment, might mitigate the visceral desire to punish, and encourage EU states to seek an accommodative settlement. However, should the perception of competence decline, and the

UK to slip into the bottom-left quadrant, passive avoidance by the EU might be the best the UK can hope for post-Brexit.

Warmth-competence stereotypes: politicians and celebrities

Studies of perceptions of broad social groups, or of entire national populations, only offer an overview of the impact of warmth-competence stereotypes on emotions and behaviours. To understand how the dimensions shape global impressions of an individual, one has to look at how a large number of respondents rate people known to all of them. This was done in a US survey, in which a representative sample of over 1,000 people were asked to rate 18 familiar celebrities and politicians. The average responses were mapped to the four-quadrant graphic (figure 5.6).

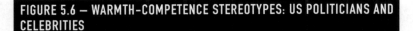

FIGURE 5.6 – WARMTH-COMPETENCE STEREOTYPES: US POLITICIANS AND CELEBRITIES

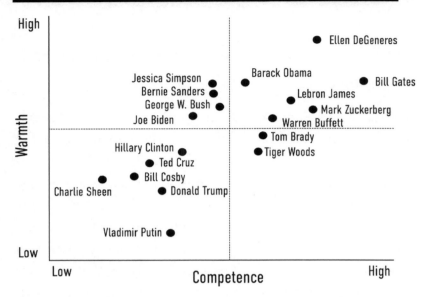

Source: Reproduced with permission from 'US Celebrity & Politician Brand Warmth & Competence Study', Fidelum Partners (2016).

Given the 2016 presidential elections were imminent at the time of the survey, it was remarkable that both presidential candidates, Donald Trump and Hillary Clinton, attracted below-average ratings for warmth and competence. Indeed, the only politician to appear in the top-right quadrant was the outgoing president, Barack Obama. In terms of intentions to vote, the authors found that warmth-competence perceptions explained fully 67% of respondents' willingness to vote for a presidential candidate, and this before consideration of any political issue, or the candidate's experience.[65]

---

65 Fidelum Partners (September 2016). 'US Celebrity & Politician Brand Warmth & Competence Study'. Retrieved from: fidelum.com/us-celebrity-politician-brand-warmth-competence-study

Warmth-competence stereotypes: professions

The results of studies of the warmth-competence perceptions of professional occupations typically reveal that most are not judged as particularly warm. The notable exceptions are the 'caring professions' – for instance, in healthcare or education. Respondents tend to rate most other jobholders as low-warmth, but with varying degrees of competence, typically depending on the perceived complexity of the work (dishwasher vs lawyer) or of the social status of the occupation (taxi driver vs CEO).[66] One such study, conducted in Germany, revealed much the same tendency. However, as job titles (like all other nouns) have a gender in the German language, separate lists were created for female (figure 5.7) and for male (figure 5.8) occupants of each of the 14 selected jobs. This made it possible to see how perceptions changed depending on the gender of the job occupant.[67]

---

66 Fiske, S. T. and Dupree, C. (2014) 'Gaining trust as well as respect in communicating to motivated audiences about science topics'. Proceedings of the National Academy of Sciences, 111, (4), 13593–13597.

67 Imhoff, R., Woelki, J., Hanke, S. and Dotsch, R. (2013) 'Warmth and competence in your face! Visual encoding of stereotype content'. Frontiers in Psychology, 4, 1–20.

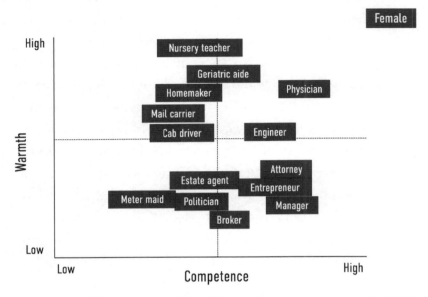

FIGURE 5.7 – WARMTH-COMPETENCE STEREOTYPES: GERMAN PROFESSIONS WHEN OCCUPIED BY WOMEN

Source: Adapted from Imhoff, Woelki, Hanke and Dotsch (2013).

A familiar pattern emerged in the data, with only the caring professions scoring highly on the warmth dimension, and the others tending to score neutral to low. Yet there is a striking observation when one compares perceptions of the same jobs when occupied by a man rather than by a woman. In every case, the male jobholder was perceived as colder than the female. The impact on the competence dimension is less clear-cut. Occupations in which success is thought to require a measure of warmth (nursery school teacher, geriatric aide, homemaker), women in these roles were perceived as more competent than men. Professions in which warmth is thought to be less essential for success (engineer, lawyer), men in these roles were perceived as more competent than women. Further study by the same researchers revealed that the mere presence of femininity was enough to improve warmth perceptions (defined as trustworthiness in the study).[68] This femininity could manifest itself, for instance, in a person's facial features, like the roundness of the shape, or smoothness of the skin.

FIGURE 5.8 – WARMTH-COMPETENCE STEREOTYPES: GERMAN PROFESSIONS WHEN OCCUPIED BY MEN

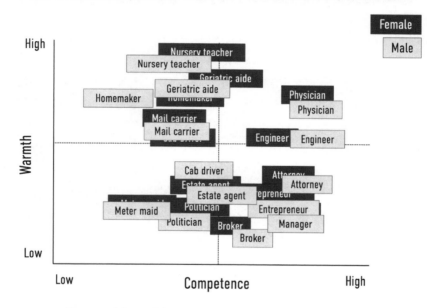

Source: Adapted from Imhoff, Woelki, Hanke and Dotsch (2013).

68 Todorov, A., Dotsch, R., Porter, J. M., Oosterhof, N. N., and Falvello, V. B. (2013) 'Validation of data-driven computational models of social perception of faces'. *Emotion*, 13 (4), 724–738.

Warmth-competence stereotypes: financial service providers

A further observation one can make about the data on the warmth-competence perceptions of professions is that people rate all occupations related to the financial services industry as cold but competent. Bankers, brokers, lawyers, managers, accountants, etc., are in the bottom right-hand corner. It gets worse: in the aftermath of the global financial crisis of 2007/08, the major US financial institutions were even perceived to be in the bottom left-hand quadrant (figure 5.9).[69] Asset managers, financial advisors and other professionals in the financial services industry face a major hurdle to being trusted – namely, that they are perceived as lacking warmth. In the best case, they are respected, even envied. Yet, beneath this accommodation, lies a deep suspicion, a hidden distrust. In the worst case, these individuals and the firms they represent are treated with contempt and rejected.

---

69 Malone, C. and Fiske, S. T. (2013) *The Human Brand: How We Relate to People, Products and Companies*. San Francisco: Jossey-Bass, 134.

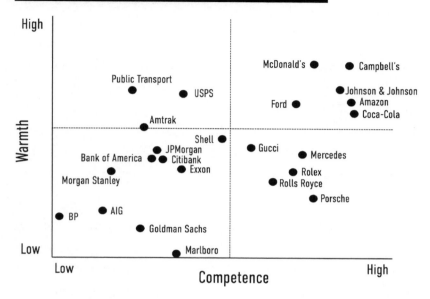

Source: Adapted with permission from *The HUMAN Brand*, Malone and Fiske (2013).

IN THE KINGDOM OF THE COLD, THE LUKEWARM IS KING

The shift to the left in perceptions of financial service professionals – the downgrade of perceptions of competence – has been one of the consequences of the 2007/08 crisis, and it has coincided with the rise in the appeal of impersonal alternatives to certified financial advisors, and to active investment managers. Human advisors have seen their market share nibbled away by so-called robo-advisors; active managers have lost assets to exchange-traded funds (ETFs). The appeal to clients of these impersonal alternatives lies mainly in their low cost, but also in their transparency and neutrality.

These products are built on formulae and algorithms that treat each client like the next. An ETF cannot 'understand' a client's needs or objectives. Similarly, no client can receive any special attention from a robo-advisor. But this is precisely the point: these formulaic products *cannot work against the client's interests either*. In a world where all financial counterparties are perceived as cold, a warmth-neutral robo-counterparty is king.

ETFs and robo-advisors are the equivalent of 'engineers' in the professions graphic (figure 5.8). They are perceived to be competent but neither warm nor cold. What motivates engineers, according to the stereotype, are things like design, product performance, efficiency, innovation, etc. In short, engineers care more about what other engineers think of their work than what end-users think. They are not working primarily in the interest of the end-users, but they do not deliberately seek to exploit them in an opportunistic manner either.

If the alternative is to transact risky business with a counterparty whom they perceive as competent but cold, clients will rather do business with 'engineers'. Ideally, though, clients would prefer as a counterparty someone whom they rate highly on both dimensions. The implication is that a financial service provider who is both warm and competent can outshine, not only other service providers, but also robo-advisors and ETFs.

SUMMARY

Two dimensions of social perception, warmth and competence, explain a major part of our impressions of others. These perceptions are not faithful representations of other people; often, in the early stage of a relationship, they just are crude stereotypes. But this does not make them any less powerful. These impressions elicit specific emotions, and these emotions give rise to specific behaviours.

For professionals in the financial services industry, especially in the aftermath of the 2007/08 financial crisis, these impressions present a major challenge, as this group is widely perceived as competent but cold. The stereotype can persist even when those judgements come from others within their own group. Germans, for example, are perceived as cold but competent, whether the person being asked is German or non-German. So fund sponsors' impression of asset managers can be similarly ambivalent, even though they operate in the same industry. This impression elicits emotions of envy and suspicion. The corresponding behaviour is begrudged accommodation in the best case, outright resentment in the worst. Faced with the option of a cold counterparty, many clients have preferred to transact their risky business with warmth-neutral robo counterparties. However, all is not lost for human professionals. They can outdo lukewarm robo-advisors and robo-asset managers. They just need to be warmer.

6 — LESSONS FROM THE MOST TRUSTED PROFESSIONS

EVIDENCE OF MEMBERSHIP of a particular group is one of the initial signals in a trustworthiness evaluation. In business, the most obvious group membership is that of the profession. This chapter will focus on the way various professional groups are perceived in terms of trustworthiness, and how that relates to the warmth-competence dimensions. Professionals in the financial services industry face a major hurdle in the trust stakes, but they are not the only ones to evoke ambivalent impressions or to be perceived as cold. Our goal in this chapter is to uncover which professional groups are trusted (or not), and why, and to show what lessons can be learned from a group that has succeeded in being perceived as both warm and competent. We will also show the implications of these high-trust relationships for both the trustor and the trustee.

A WORLDWIDE RANKING OF TRUST IN PROFESSIONS

The German market research company, GfK Verein, conducts a biannual survey of trust in professions.[70] In its most recent poll, which interviewed approximately 30,000 consumers on five continents, it found some notable consistency in the way 32 pre-determined professional groups were perceived around the world. For example, 'taxi driver' was the least-trusted group in South Africa, and ranked in the lower half of the global list. In Indonesia people expressed suspicion of the category 'priest'. The lack of trust in this group was palpable at the global level, too, where it ranked seven professions below taxi driver. At the bottom of the global list, as well as those in 22 of the 27 countries surveyed, 'politician' ranked as the least trusted. Financial service providers reached middling trust values in the global survey – better than retailers, but not as good as judges. In European countries, they were fifth from bottom. The survey's authors attributed this to Europeans' continued preoccupation with the financial crisis.

Politicians are not trusted...

Warmth-competence perceptions help to explain these low trust rankings. Politician, which was the least trusted of the 32 occupations in the US sample of the GfK Verein survey, likewise scores poorly on both dimensions of US warmth-competence

---

70 GfK Verein. Gesellschaft fuer Konsum-, Markt- und Absatzforschung e.V. *Trust in Professions 2016 – From firefighters to politicians.*

surveys. 'Taxi driver', too, figures in the bottom left-hand quadrant of warmth-competence mappings, though warmer than politician. Both groups, therefore, suffer from negative stereotypes regarding their trustworthiness. Brokers, bankers, lawyers, and others involved in the financial services industry, typically attract more favourable perceptions of competence. So, even though they are seen as lacking warmth, overall trust perceptions tend to be more favourable.

On the opposing end of GfK Verein's trust scale, one finds occupations such as teacher (most-trusted in Turkey and Indonesia), farmer (most-trusted in Kenya and Nigeria) and paramedics (most trusted in Switzerland, Japan and the UK). Nurse ranked second overall and topped the list in South Korea. However, at the top of the global list, and of those in 16 of the 27 countries surveyed, was firefighter.

...but firefighters *are* trusted

Why are firefighters so universally trusted? Firstly, the entry requirements for firefighters are assumed to be very exacting. Not only must they master increasingly complex equipment under the most challenging of situations, they must also have thorough knowledge of types of fire, building infrastructure, and first aid. In addition, they must be able to meet demanding physical fitness benchmarks. Hence, one might assume that someone who is employed as a firefighter is perceived to be competent in that role.

Firefighters also score highly on the perceived warmth dimension. Remember, being described as warm means that targets are perceived as having the interests of their 'clients', i.e.

the people they protect from the flames, ahead of their own. The public likely believes this to be the case in the firefighting profession. Consider a theoretical situation in which a child is trapped on the second floor of a burning building. Who doubts that firefighters would be prepared to put themselves in harm's way to protect that child from harm? This is the reason we are unsurprised by reports of heroic firefighters putting their lives on the line to rescue trapped disaster victims. This is the kind of thing firefighters do. They are also one of the 'caring professions'.

Our explanation for the trust accorded to firefighters across the globe is largely intuitive because no research we are aware of has looked closely at the public's actual experience of firefighters – only its perception of them (mercifully, few people have regular contact with them on a professional basis.) Yet, there is another professional group that has also been able to achieve the 'magic double' – a high score in both warmth and competence – and has been the subject of much scientific investigation: physicians.

The warmth-competence data from the survey published in 2014 showed that doctors in the US enjoyed a high standing as a trusted professional group.[71] Already by then, however, this reputation had started to suffer due to several high-profile scandals concerning negligent misdiagnoses or delayed diagnoses (competence), and the taking of bribes and kickbacks to overprescribe unsuitable drugs (warmth). In the 2016 GfK Verein poll, for example, doctors only ranked fourth on a worldwide basis, behind teachers, nurses and, of course,

---

71 Fiske, S. T. and Dupree, C. (2014) 'Gaining trust as well as respect in communicating to motivated audiences about science topics'. Proceedings of the National Academy of Sciences, 111, (4), 13593–13597.

firefighters. In European countries, they were placed just sixth. But there nevertheless exists ample historical data concerning the implications of high-trust relationships for both physicians and their patients, and about what might have been the drivers of the earlier, more favourable perception.

TRUST IN PATIENT–DOCTOR RELATIONSHIPS

Trust has been shown to affect a host of important behaviours and attitudes in the patient-doctor relationship.[72] It affects, for example, the willingness of a patient to seek care in the first place. People who feel unwell are more likely to consult a doctor if they trust that individual. Once at the doctor, people are more likely to disclose sensitive information about their symptoms and lifestyle to someone they trust. Armed with this information, the physician is better able to make a diagnosis and to propose the most suitable treatments. Patients are more likely to submit to the treatment proposed by a trusted doctor and to adhere to it over its full course. This patient discipline contributes to successful outcomes in those medical treatments. One longitudinal study of trust between physicians and diabetic patients, for example, revealed improvements in patients' mental and physical quality

---

72 Hall, M. A., Dugan, E., Zheng, B. and Mishra, A. K. (2001) 'Trust in Physicians and Medical Institutions: What Is It, Can It Be Measured, and Does It Matter?' *Milbank Quarterly*, 79: 613–639. doi: 10.1111/1468-0009.00223.

of life, and greater levels of patient satisfaction, associated with higher levels of trust.[73]

It has also been documented that doctors who are perceived as warm are less likely to be sued for malpractice.[74] On the face of it, malpractice lawsuits ought to be all about competence, or lack of it, not warmth. Yet, it is the cold doctors who are most often sued when medical errors occur, not the warm ones. It appears that when patients perceive the physician's mistakes to have been well-intended, they are more inclined to forgive than to seek legal redress. Not only are the patients of trusted doctors involved in fewer disputes with their healthcare providers, they are also less likely to seek a second opinion, are more likely to stay with the same doctor over time, and are more likely to recommend their doctor to others. So these high-trust relationships bring tangible advantages for the patient's health as well as for the physician's livelihood.

A parallel between doctors and money managers?

Most money managers can only dream of the kind of client relationships doctors enjoy. They would want nothing more than to be able to replace the word 'patient' with 'fund client' in the above research conclusions. Their desired objective is precisely to have clients come to them when they need care,

73 Lee, Y., and Lin, J. L. (2011) 'How much does trust really matter? A study of the longitudinal effects of trust and decision-making preferences on diabetic patient outcomes'. *Patient Education and Counseling*, 85 (3), 406–412.

74 Levinson W., Roter, D. L., Mullooly, J. P., Dull, V. T., Frankel, R. M. (1997) 'Physician-patient communication. The relationship with malpractice claims among primary care physicians and surgeons'. *JAMA*, 277 (7), 553–559.

i.e. when they need to delegate asset management. They want their clients to speak openly and honestly, not only about their organisation's stated investment objectives, but also about the equally important but often unspoken personal career goals. They want their clients to submit to the financial 'treatments' they propose, and to adhere to the asset allocation strategies in a disciplined fashion over the entire investment cycle. Finally, they want their clients to remain with them, and to recommend them to others. So, money managers would certainly like to emulate doctors – but is it really possible, or is this relationship unique in some way?

One might reasonably ask whether the trust expressed in physicians is really trust at all. When a patient consults a doctor, the former is possibly in a state of emotional, if not physical, distress. In most cases, the patient will know significantly less about medicine than the doctor, so an information asymmetry will exist which might add to the patient's unease. One could argue, therefore, that any subsequent expression of trust in the doctor is nothing more than a psychological coping mechanism in response to anxiety caused by illness and by informational disadvantage.

Such a configuration is unlikely to exist between fund clients and their money managers. To begin with, sponsors and investment consultants are typically as well-trained and as well-informed as the asset managers they evaluate. There is still a risk for clients, of course but, as they are more knowledgeable about the hazards of investing, their perception of the risks is diminished. Without risk, there is no need for trust. Indeed, the research evidence also suggests that the emergence of trust is unrelated to risk/benefit perceptions when people are knowledgeable about the dangers they face.[75] For dangers, about which people do not feel knowledgeable, trust is very strongly related to risk/benefit perceptions. For example, a skyscraper architect might be persuaded to live on the 50th floor of a building without necessarily trusting the construction company. Yet, the same architect might not feel comfortable living within the radius of a nuclear power station without the assurances of a trusted developer.

If the existence of trust in a client-provider relationship relied on the characteristics of the client (physical or emotional distress, lack of knowledge, or perception of elevated risks), it would be imprudent to draw close parallels with patient-doctor relationships. Yet, research has shown that whether a patient trusts a doctor has very little to do with the patient. Demographic factors such as age, ethnicity, gender, socio-economic status, or education, are poorly correlated, even when the patient shares those demographics with the doctor. The state of the patient's health has little or no impact on trust. Even patients in relatively good health can be disposed to trust their doctors. Similarly, the length of time a patient has known a doctor, or the frequency of visits they have made, although positive, is only weakly related to trust. This suggests that trust can emerge from the very first encounter. It seems that every patient enters treatment encounters with, at least, the *capacity* to trust. Whether they do thereafter depends almost entirely on the doctor's subsequent behaviour. It is possible to draw a parallel because the trust relationship depends largely on the characteristics of the service provider, not of the client.

---

75 Siegrist, M., Cvetkovich, G. and Roth, C. (2000) 'Salient value similarity, social trust, and risk/benefit perception'. *Risk Analysis.*, 20, 353–362.

How do doctors win trust?

The strongest predictors of trust are physicians' communication style and their interpersonal skills. For instance, doctors who spend more time talking with patients, who laugh and share anecdotes, are more trusted than those whose consultations are shorter and more business-like. Effective communication among physicians also involves active listening. This means concentrating fully on the speaker, using verbal and non-verbal information to try to understand what he is saying, and providing gestural and verbal feedback to demonstrate that one has understood. Active listening encourages patients to talk and share valuable information. It has also been suggested that the tone of the physician's voice is a better predictor of the likelihood of a future malpractice lawsuit than the frequency of that doctor's errors. This holds true even when listeners do not know what the doctor is talking about; the voice's intonation, pitch and rhythm alone reveal whether doctors sound dominant, or whether they sound concerned.[76] All listeners, whether they are the patient or not, are particularly sensitive to these vocal signals.

Doctors are also more trusted if they take an active interest in the wider well-being of their patients, not just in the ailment that bought them into the practice on that day. This holistic approach requires gathering information about the patient's wider environment, and often involves educating patients so

---

76 Ambady, N., Laplante, D., Nguyen, T., Rosenthal, R., Chaumeton, N., Levinson, W. (2002) 'Surgeons' tone of voice: a clue to malpractice history'. *Surgery*, 132 (1), 5–9.

that they are well prepared for what the visit, their illness, their medical predispositions, or even their age has in store for them.

Even for doctors, trust is a product of a high score on both dimensions of perception, warmth and competence. But, in contrast to asset managers and many other financial professions, they do not spend much time reminding their customers of their competence. Doctors are not often asked where they graduated, or where they worked previously. They are not challenged for the percentage of patients they cured of a given pathology over the past one, three and five years. This allows physicians to spend a far greater proportion of their time conveying warmth: "How are you feeling?"; "Where does it hurt?"; "Let me help you." In the caring professions, skill is not measured by the longevity of the patient, but by the energy directed at the task. This is the reason doctors are more often trusted than not.

Another factor that might play a role in physicians' high trust ratings is the Hippocratic Oath. There are actually not many places in the world where doctors still swear an oath, least of all the original version. More commonly, newly qualified medical students make a more contemporary promise to 'do no harm', or to uphold ethical standards. Others swear nothing at all. Yet many patients think they adhere to a moral code of conduct. Such a code is a commitment to put the patient's interests first – a promise to be warm. Social sanctions, like 'shaming', await medical professionals who breach moral codes, even those who act legally. If patients believe doctors are bound by a code of conduct, then the medical profession might indeed have an important head-start, in the trust stakes, over professionals in other domains. There is no evidence to our knowledge that belief in a code is a predictor for trust and, even if there was, there is nothing to prevent money managers from introducing their own oath. Indeed, many professions already do insist on a signed or public declaration of adherence to their industry's ethical code.

MONEY MANAGERS SHOULD LEARN FROM DOCTORS

Some recent research into the impact of a high trust in delegated fund management relationships has suggested that the lessons from the medical profession can be generalised.[77] The research sought to understand why fund clients continue to pay such high fees despite considerable evidence that the vast majority of asset managers perform rather poorly relative to their benchmarks. In an efficient market, management fees should fall to cost under these conditions, but this does not happen. The study's authors developed a model of delegated portfolio management based on trust. Even though managers underperform on average, the researchers contend, clients under the trust condition might still prefer to delegate rather than to invest on their own.

A trusted manager has the effect of alleviating some of the client's anxiety about the riskiness of any given investment. This enables clients to take on board more risk than they would have felt comfortable shouldering alone. This supposition is supported by the empirical data on retail investors: after taking

---

77 Gennaioli, N., Shleifer, A. and Visny, R. (2015) 'Money Doctors'. *The Journal of Finance*, 70, 91–114.

into consideration variation due to demographic profile, those retail investors who use financial advisors tend to hold riskier portfolios than those who do not pay for advice. Over the long run, an investor who accepts more risk could be expected to earn higher returns. Hence, the high-trust relationship brings tangible advantages for the fund client as well as for the asset manager.

The advantages of delegation in fund management do not end there. The model also predicts that investors would be more likely to remain with a trusted manager. Just as in the patient-doctor relationship, this is important for clients' positive long-run outcomes because it saves them significant administrative costs associated with the frequent search and selection of alternative managers, and the transitioning of assets to them. There is little evidence to suggest the average fund sponsor has any timing ability when it comes to hiring and firing managers, so a constant churn is not in their interests. It is an unfortunate truth, but even if average fund clients were presented with a choice of solidly performing managers, many would still underperform because of the tendency to switch from manager to manager at the worst possible moment. By remaining with a trusted manager, clients avoid the switching costs. Once again, trust brings benefits for both parties.

Finally, a trusted manager should expect to have fewer disputes. Clients are more likely to be indulgent of disappointing outcomes if they believe the actions of the manager were well-intentioned. There should also be fewer discussions about fees. In the eyes of the client, a cold manager *earns* fees; a warm manager *deserves* them.

SUMMARY

Asset managers can learn from the professions that consistently achieve high trust ratings with the public. One such trusted group are physicians, for whom a significant body of data exists to describe the antecedents and consequences of that trust. The strongest predictors of trust in physicians are their communication style and interpersonal skills. Talking with patients, laughing and sharing anecdotes, and employing a concerned tone of voice, are all elements of this interpersonal skill. Active listening also encourages patients to share the kind of crucial information that allows physicians to make more accurate diagnoses. Doctors are also more trusted if they take an active interest in the wider well-being of their patients. These are all skills that financial professionals can develop and employ.

If the lessons of the doctor-patient relationship can be replicated in the financial services industry, the benefits of greater trust between money managers and clients are multiple. More openness and honesty about clients' needs would allow managers to propose the most appropriate solutions and thereby serve them better. The greater client tolerance for risk, when accompanied by a trusted manager, ought to enhance returns over the long run. Finally, improved client fidelity would save clients' money, by avoiding costly search and selection, and enhance managers' reputation.

7 — THE FOUNDATIONS OF INTERPERSONAL TRUST

HENRY, THE INVESTOR, wasn't keen on accepting a stockbroker's invitation to share a taxi – a sales pitch for a whole mile, he thought. He was wrong. The stockbroker neither mentioned his firm nor any stock. He merely unknotted his tie and stuffed it in his jacket pocket. "It's not my favourite," he said, "but my son chose it for my birthday, so I have to wear it." He continued: "My boy's ten. That's about the age when sons suddenly realise their fathers are not superhuman after all. Mine thinks I'm a loser." One mile later, Henry had decided that he quite liked this stockbroker.

The events described above took place as the taxi wound its way through Hong Kong's busy financial district. In the space of ten minutes, Henry's impression of the stockbroker had moved from mild distaste to guarded appreciation. What happened? Admittedly, the bar was set very low for the broker; that he wasn't the blinkered, sales-orientated bore Henry had imagined was already a positive point. But there was much more taking place. Without being conscious of it, Henry had been looking for signals that would inform him about what a business relationship with this man would be like, and he found some.

His informality, his family orientation, his self-deprecation, were all elements that Henry might have been attentive to. That both he and Henry were foreigners in China might also have played a role, as they recognised themselves as part of the local outgroup, and imagined they shared some Anglo-Saxon values. Whatever the signals were, Henry made an instant judgement about the man's warmth. Thus far, he had no clues as to his competence as a stockbroker, but his fellow passenger belonged to a professional group that is stereotypically competent, so that was a start. This is not trust, of course, but a trusting state of mind had begun to emerge. If Henry had a risky decision to make, he might be inclined to allow this stockbroker to advise him.

The foundations for interpersonal trust are established during the very first encounter. Right from the outset, our cognitive system will start to search for cues or signals from the unknown other that it associates with the state of mind called trust. These can be social cues, like the other's words and gestures, or the words and gestures of third parties. Sometimes the cognitive system 'outsources' some of its work to the physical environment, and takes its cues from the sights, sounds, odours and sensations in the surroundings. The presence (or absence) of these cues influences the way information is processed during the encounter and, therefore, the judgements about whether we believe a new person is trustworthy or not. Once a cue is recognised, any others that are consistent with it become more salient. So, the process is self-reinforcing. The judgement can take place within a fraction of a second, without our consent, acknowledgement, or even our recognition. This chapter will therefore present examples of these social and physical cues, and show how they operate as catalysts for interpersonal trust.

THE LOVE DRUG

Experiments have revealed that one method of predisposing someone to trust is the administration of the hormone oxytocin, otherwise known as the 'love drug'. Oxytocin is manufactured in the brain and secreted by the pituitary gland. It plays an important role in two key female reproductive functions: childbirth and breastfeeding. In fairness to those in the medical profession, the process is a little more complicated than we will describe it here, and trust itself is too complex a behaviour to be resolved by a single isolated molecule, but it acts to reduce a (very human) wariness of proximity with unknown others. It enhances sociality,[78,79,80,81] cooperation,[82,83] and the sense of

---

78 Israel, S., Weisel, O., Ebstein, R. P., and Bornstein, G. (2012) 'Oxytocin, but not vasopressin, increases both parochial and universal altruism'. *Psychoneuroendocrinology*, 37, (8), 1341–1344. doi.org/10.1016/j. psyneuen.2012.02.001

79 Kosfeld, M. et al. (2005) 'Oxytocin increases trust in human'. *Nature*, 435, 673–676. doi:10.1038/nature03701.

80 Radke, S. and De Bruijn, E. R. A. (2012) 'The other side of the coin: oxytocin decreases the adherence to fairness norms'. *Frontiers in Human Neuroscience*, 6, 1–7. doi:10.3389/fnhum.2012.00193.

81 Zak, P. J., Stanton, A. A. and Ahmadi, S. (2007) 'Oxytocin Increases Generosity in Humans'. PLOS ONE 11, 1128.

82 Bartz, J. A. et al. (2010) 'Oxytocin Selectively Improves Empathic Accuracy'. *Psychological Science*, 21 (10), 1426–1428. doi.org/10.1177/0956797610383439

83 Declerck, C. H., Boone, C. and Kiyonari, T. (2010). 'Oxytocin and

affiliation,[84,85] all of which are helpful for the establishment of trust. The outcome, for instance, is that should a woman unexpectedly go into labour without her family nearby, she may be emboldened to grab the first available taxi driver to help her. And once the baby is born, she will quickly be able to develop an intimate relationship with it.

Oxytocin is produced naturally in the hypothalamus, but biochemists have been able to synthesise it for commercial purposes. It is therefore readily available in the form of a nasal spray from online stores, and it is this that scientists have used in multiple studies designed to measure its impact on trusting behaviour. The results have demonstrated that the administration of oxytocin significantly increases an individual's willingness to take social risks.[86] Oxytocin is not unique in this respect; Hedione, a chemically synthesized odorant with a jasmine-like smell, has a similar effect.[87] These behaviours result not only in closer social interactions, but also in a tendency for counterparties to

cooperation under conditions of uncertainty: The modulating role of incentives and social information'. *Hormones and Behavior*, 57 (3), 368–374. doi. org/10.1016/j.yhbeh.2010.01.006

84 Feldman, R. (2012) 'Oxytocin and social affiliation in humans'. *Hormones and Behavior*, 61 (3), 380–391. doi.org/10.1016/j.yhbeh.2012.01.008

85 Smith et al. (2013) 'Problems with measuring peripheral oxytocin: Can the data on oxytocin and human behavior be trusted?'. *Neuroscience & Biobehavioral Reviews*, 37 (8), 1485–1492. doi.org/10.1016/j.neubiorev.2013.04.018

86 Kosfeld, M., Heinrichs, M., Zak, P.J., Fischbacher, U. and Fehr, E. (2005) 'Oxytocin increases trust in humans'. *Nature*, 435, 673–676. doi: 10.1038/nature03701.

87 Berger, S., Hatt, H. and Ockenfels, A. (2017) 'Exposure to Hedione Increases Reciprocity in Humans'. *Frontiers in Behavoiral Neuroscience*, 11 (79). doi: 10.3389/fnbeh.2017.00079.

reciprocate expressions of trust with trusting behaviour of their own. The consequence of so-called 'social odours', therefore, is to increase the benefits of social interactions for both parties.

Before we continue, it is essential that we stress that we do not suggest exploiting the neurological effects of a synthesised hormone or odorant in a business relationship. We discuss the 'love drug' to, firstly, demonstrate how deeply rooted our decision to trust is. It takes place without our being conscious of it, and without the subsequently trusted person having said or done anything to merit it. Secondly, we want to restate the importance of trust for social interactions, like cooperation. Finally, we want to mark out the ethical limits to efforts to win trust. Clearly, diffusing chemical vapours into the room ahead of a business encounter without the other person's knowledge would be immoral. But, at least, the choice is clear: a drug-free room is the ethical option. In the case of many physical and social cues, no such choice exists. Whatever cue is present (or absent) will be associated with trust. The only choice one has is to make it deliberate, or to leave it to chance. There is no cue-free environment.

TRUST BY PHYSICAL CUES

Physical cues in the environment include obvious features, like temperature and odour. But they also include elements such as brightness, décor, orderliness, etc. We present some examples where the evidence is most abundant.

Physical cues: temperature

You and a colleague are invited to attend a lecture by a visiting financial consultant. Near the doorway of the conference room, the organisers have provided a table with light refreshments. You serve yourself a hot coffee; your colleague prefers a chilled soda. At the end of the short lecture, the organisers circulate feedback forms and ask attendees to kindly note their impressions of the presentation – both the content and the presenter. One question specifically asks delegates to rate the lecturer on qualities such as empathy, inclusiveness and approachability, i.e. on characteristics typically related to the warmth dimension. As you and you colleague watched the same presentation, one might imagine the responses would be similar. Yet there is evidence to suggest they will be different in a systematic way. You, together with all the other attendees who selected hot beverages on the way in, probably rated the lecturer as warmer than those who opted for chilled drinks.

Psychologists have long theorised that infants establish a mental link between the psychological warmth of their early caregivers – e.g. their generosity, kindness, etc. – and their physical warmth. Indeed, in mammals, the satisfaction of an infant's primary needs, nourishment and security, requires the close physical proximity of the caregiver. Without it, the infant's social development, if not its very survival, could be threatened. The link between psychological and physical warmth is so strong it has been suggested that they could be substitutable. This means that a person who lacked psychological warmth might unknowingly compensate for it by seeking physical warmth. An example would be taking a hot bath as a remedy for loneliness.[88]

Theories such as these have encouraged scientists to explore the possibility of deliberately activating this mental link – stimulating the feeling of psychological warmth towards a stranger by simultaneously exposing experimental subjects to a source of physical warmth. In one study[89] a laboratory assistant accompanied individual subjects in an elevator from the lobby to the fourth floor of the building where an experiment was to be conducted. On the way, he casually asked each of them to briefly hold his coffee cup so he could note the subject's name, the date, and time on a clipboard. Unbeknownst to both the subject, and the laboratory assistant, there was no experiment on the fourth floor. In fact, the experiment was already over by the time the elevator reached its destination, because the scientists only wanted to observe the impact of holding the cup on subjects' perceptions of the assistant.

The researchers had divided the subjects into two groups: half would be asked to hold a cup containing hot coffee during the short elevator ride; the other half would be asked to hold an iced coffee. As hypothesised, subjects who were briefly exposed to the hot coffee cup perceived the laboratory assistant to be significantly friendlier, more caring etc. than those in the iced-coffee group. These findings support the view that serving hot

---

88 Shalev, I. and Bargh, J. A. (2015) 'On the association between loneliness and physical warmth-seeking through bathing: Reply to Donnellan et al. (2014) and three further replications of Bargh and Shalev (2012) study 1'. *Emotion*, 15 (1), 120–123.

89 Williams, L. E. and Bargh, J. A. (2008) 'Experiencing physical warmth promotes interpersonal warmth'. *Science*, 322, 606–607.

drinks during a business meeting is useful for eliciting favourable first perceptions. What if one has no hot drinks to offer? The mental link between psychological warmth and physical warmth is so strong that it is sufficient for people to *imagine* themselves holding a hot or cold beverage for the effect to materialise.[90]

Physical cues: odour

There are some natural odours everyone seems to like. For instance, across distant countries and diverse cultures, there is almost universal appreciation for the smell of vanilla, and of citrus fruits. Another natural odour that is always near the top of those global lists is peppermint. Not only do we like it, but studies have shown that in the presence of a peppermint scent we are more motivated and alert, less anxious and fatigued,[91] demonstrate improved concentration[92] and memory,[93] make

90 Macrae, C. N., Raj, R. S., Best, S. B., Christian, B. M. and Miles, L. K. (2013) 'Imagined sensory experiences can shape person perception: It's a matter of visual perspective'. *Journal of Experimental Social Psychology*, 49, 595–598. doi: 10.1016/j.jesp.2012.10.002.

91 Sakamoto, R., Minoura, K., Usui, A., Ishizuka, Y. and Kanba, S. (2005) 'Effectiveness of aroma on work efficiency: lavender aroma during recesses prevents deterioration of work performance'. *Chemical Senses*, 30, 683–691. doi: 10.1093/chemse/bji061.

92 Raudenbush, B., Grayhem, R., Sears, T. and Wilson, I. (2009) 'Effects of peppermint and cinnamon odor administration on simulated driving alertness, mood and workload'. *North American Journal of Psychology*, 11, 245–256.

93 Moss, M., Hewitt, S., Moss, L. and Wesnes, K. (2008) 'Modulation of cognitive performance and mood by aromas of peppermint and ylang-ylang'. *International Journal of Neuroscience*, 118, 59–77.doi:10.1080/00207450601042094.

fewer errors on clerical tasks,[94] and even perform better athletically.[95] It appears, however, that none of peppermint's remarkable abilities are effective in encouraging interpersonal trust. In experiments involving the Trust Game[96] there was no significant difference in the trusting behaviour of players exposed to the peppermint scent and those in the no-scent, control group. Although players certainly found the scent agreeable – and its performance-enhancing properties might have allowed them to quickly conclude that collaboration was the economically optimal strategy – they tended not to collaborate more. There was one odour, however, that did prompt a significant increase in trusting behaviour: lavender.[97] Although both peppermint and lavender are universally well-liked, it is apparently not the pleasantness or the likeability of a scent that contributes to interpersonal trust; it is the lavender.

Physical cues: the surroundings

Observers can draw a wealth of information from spaces that people occupy. Rooms where people live, work and sleep, leave behind what is known as *behavioural residue*. These are traces of

---

94 Barker, S. et al. (2003) 'Improved Performance on Clerical Tasks Associated with Administration of Peppermint Odor'. *Perceptual and Motor Skills*. 97 (3), 1007–1010.

95 Raudenbush, B., Corley, N., and Eppich, W. (2001) 'Enhancing athletic performance through the administration of peppermint odor'. *Journal of Sport and Exercise Psychology*, 23, 156–160.

96 See Annex 1.

97 Sellaro, R., Van Dijk, W. W., Paccani, C. R., Hommel, B. and Colzato, L. S. (2015) 'A question of scent: lavender aroma promotes interpersonal trust'. *Frontiers in Psychology*, 5, 1486. doi: 10.3389/fpsyg.2014.01486.

what others have done there (a crumpled beanbag and a book with a page marker in the middle), what they are planning to do there (an unopened wine bottle and two clean wine glasses), and what they do elsewhere (movie ticket stubs and a pair of 3D glasses). People are remarkably adept at recognising this behavioural residue, and at drawing inferences from it about the occupant's character. Research in the field of zero-acquaintance impression formation (typically this means impressions formed after a very brief exposure to the target individual) has revealed that not only does there tend to be a consensus when observers independently gather this 'residual' information about someone, but also that the inferences made tend to be rather accurate.

In one study, test subjects were invited to rate office workers following a brief inspection of their personal workspaces. Any obvious clues to the identity of the occupant, like photos, were carefully concealed ahead of the visit. The results revealed a significant degree of consensus about the meaning of various physical cues in the working space, especially with regards to the occupant's openness, conscientiousness and extraversion. The researchers also discovered that these impressions were remarkably accurate, given that observers had no physical contact at all with the occupants.[98] What were the physical cues? Impressions of 'openness' were left by the distinctiveness of the workplace, the decoration, the quantity of magazines, and the quantity and diversity of books. 'Conscientiousness' was signalled by the orderliness of the space, its cleanliness, and the absence of clutter. In contrast, a cluttered workspace, bright

---

98 Gosling, S. D. et al., (2002) 'A Room with a Cue'. *Journal of Personality and Social Psychology*, 82 (3), 379–98.

and colourful décor, and an unconventional organisation, were associated with 'extraversion'.

TRUST BY SOCIAL CUES

If a stranger is like us, it is more likely that we will trust him. This plain truth has its roots in our own egocentricity. Quite simply, we all prefer to see ourselves as being gifted with a raft of admirable qualities: honesty, fidelity, morality, industry and, of course, trustworthiness. If, therefore, an unknown person reminds us of ourselves because of the way he looks, dresses, talks, etc., we tend to attribute to that person the same qualities we attribute to ourselves. What is striking in this context is that we often do not consciously recognise any similarity. Nonetheless, the initial stage towards a trusting relationship can be set at a glance.

Social cues: name similarity

"A person's name is to that person, the sweetest, most important sound in any language", according to Dale Carnegie in his bestselling book, *How To Win Friends And Influence People*.[99] Indeed, one's self is so central to one's perception of what is 'good' or 'desirable', the entire name is not even required; the individual letters in one's name will do. At least among people who like themselves, we display a disproportional preference

---

99 Carnegie, D. (2006) *How to Win Friends and Influence People*. New York: Pocket Books.

for the letters in our own name over all the other letters in the alphabet.[100] This means that if a product or service has a name that includes the same letters as the evaluator's name, he will like it more. Evaluators are also more likely to comply with a request from someone who shares their name.[101] So reliable is this name-letter effect, the absence of this preference is used in a measure for narcissism.

Social cues: facial similarity

One of the most obvious similarities one will detect in another person is any facial resemblance. In one experiment, which was designed so that test subjects would not be conscious of any resemblance, participants in a trust game were given the opportunity to see a picture of their counterparties.[102] More specifically, the trustors in the game were shown a picture of the supposed trustees to test the impact of different faces on their trusting behaviour. Behind the scenes, however, the pictures did not faithfully correspond to the faces of the trustees, or of anyone else's for that matter, because they were all artificially constructed using computerised morphing technology. Each face was a composition of two separate individuals, morphed together to create an almost natural appearance.

100 Nuttin, J. M. (1985) 'Narcissism beyond Gestalt and awareness: The name–letter effect'. *European Journal of Social Psychology*, 15 (3), 353–361. doi:10.1002/ejsp.2420150309.

101 Cialdini, R. B. (2001) *Influence: Science and Practice* (4th ed.). Needham Heights, MA: Allyn & Bacon.

102 DeBruine, L. M. (2002) 'Facial resemblance enhances trust'. Proceedings of the Royal Society B: Biological Sciences, 269, 1307–1312.

For the subjects in the control group, neither of the two individuals in the morphed composite image were familiar, so the picture was genuinely that of a stranger. In the experimental group, however, the morphed images contained a significant proportion of the test subject's own face. Without them being aware of it, the trustors in the second group stared at faces that were – by as much as half – essentially self-portraits. The consequence was a significant increase in trusting behaviour. A final test to see whether the incidence of trusting behaviour was due to non-conscious self-recognition, or merely to a general sense of familiarity (that person looks vaguely familiar, but I can't quite figure out where from), the study included a third test whereby the subjects were shown images of (moderately) famous people. Here, there was no increase in trusting behaviour. So, it appears the trusting effect was likely due to the unwitting self-recognition.

The morphed-face study was published in 2002. At that time, the opportunities to exploit its findings, benevolently or otherwise, were limited. In the meantime, however, the proliferation of cameras in the public domain, face-recognition technology, social networking and online financial services, mean that these opportunities have mushroomed. Financial services firms now know what we look like. The internet is littered with pictures of our faces – either deliberately on our online profiles, or unsuspectingly on someone else's. Our banks recover a snapshot of our face each time we withdraw cash from an ATM. At the same time, the growth in online financial services means that we increasingly communicate with our bank, financial advisor and insurer via their web page or application. Those online interfaces frequently portray images, ostensibly of their friendly, smiling customer services personnel. It would now be very easy for an institution to present each individual client with a face that is to a large extent a self-portrait, and to capture the increase in trusting behaviour to market their product. We hasten to add that using morphed faces to increase sales crosses the moral line.

Social cues: gestural similarity

It is well-documented that a person in conversation with someone they like or admire will involuntarily mimic that person's physical gestures or mannerisms. For instance, if the admired person should lean forward, fold his arms, or cross his legs, the admirer will find himself spontaneously doing the same.[103] This inadvertent behaviour seems to be appreciated by the admired because they tend to like better (non-consciously, of course) those who mimic their physical gestures. Therefore, gestural mimicry is effective in promoting warmth evaluations. In one study of this effect, a restaurant waitress was instructed to verbally mimic half her customers by repeating their orders back to them. With the size of the subsequent tips as a guide, the researchers concluded that mimicry had a significant impact on diners' appreciation of the waitress.

The ease with which people can learn to mimic the gestures of another person is often overlooked in references to scientific studies. The people who are charged with the task of mimicking test subjects in these studies are not extensively trained for the role. They might just be a group of uninitiated students who

---

103 Chartrand, T. L., and Bargh, J. A. (1999) 'The chameleon effect: The perception-behavior link and social interaction'. *Journal of Personality and Social Psychology*, 76, 893–910.

have been roped into the exercise. They will be briefly instructed how to mimic simple physical gestures. For example, if the test subjects scratch their ears, yawn, stretch, push their glasses up on their noses, or perform any of a range of common gestures, they are told to repeat it with a 30-second delay. It takes no more than a half-hour of practice to get the hang of it. The test subjects are unaware of the experimental objectives. They are merely told that they will have a conversation with someone, and are warned that this other person will try to convince them of a certain point of view. The results of these conversations are remarkable. Not only are those exposed to the gestural mimicry more convinced of the arguments put forward by their interlocutors, none of them recognise that their gestures have been mimicked. These results are the product of just 30 minutes of pre-conversation practice.

Social cues: food similarity

Dining is an essential part of social and cultural life. The event itself, and the kind of food served, has the effect of bringing people together, and of signalling adherence to social and cultural norms. The implications of food for trust, however, go further than simple in-group signalling. Eating the same food as another person has the effect of bringing consumers closer and increasing liking, which leads to increased trust and cooperation.[104] This finding owes something to the gestural mimicry described above – people even mimic the *amount* of

---

104 Woolley, K. and Fishbach, A. (2016) 'A recipe for friendship: Similar food consumption promotes trust and cooperation'. *Journal of Consumer Psychology*, 30 (8), 683–91. doi.org/10.1016/j.jcps.2016.06.003

food that others choose.[105] One might also argue that making the same menu choice as a stranger sends the signal that one shares the same preferences, and is therefore similar. Yet, in a study where food was assigned, i.e. no preference signalling was possible, consumption of similar food nonetheless increased closeness and cooperation. Furthermore, the research suggested there was something special about similar food consumption that made it a more powerful signal of similarity than some other forms of visual resemblance, like shirt colour. This liking and trust also extended to product advertising. Study participants exposed to non-food product testimonials also expressed greater trust in the products, and liked the advertisers more, when they and the advertisers ate the same food.

Social cues: communication style

The communication style of an interlocutor, as we have already discussed in the context of patient-doctor relationships, has important implications for the emergence and development of trust. Researchers have gone even further and have theorised that four specific elements in the communication style could convey information that affect both perceptions of warmth and competence: thanking, apologising, bragging and blaming.

All four elements carry information about where responsibility lies for positive or negative outcomes. Bragging about successes, and blaming others for failures, make the communicator appear competent. However, bragging (accepting credit) and blaming (conferring blame) are perceived as selfish, and will tend to affect

---

105 Johnston, L. (2002) 'Behavioral Mimicry and Stigmatization'. *Social Cognition*, 20, (1), 18–35. doi.org/10.1521/soco.20.1.18.20944

perceptions of the interlocutor's warmth negatively. Thanking others for positive outcomes (conferring credit), and apologising for negative outcomes (accepting blame), downplays competence. Such gestures are perceived as generous and, therefore, affect warmth perceptions positively.[106]

People are more prone to 'brag and blame' than they are to 'thank and apologise', especially in the financial services industry. This might be because the finance professionals underweight the importance of warmth perceptions in their clients' choice of service provider. Yet, this research suggests that being seen to confer credit and to accept blame should have a positive impact on trust. Another, as yet untested but possibly more palatable, approach might be to be seen to thank and apologise for outcomes that are unrelated to core competence. In this way, one might be able enhance one's warmth perception without incurring a corresponding loss to the perception of competence.

Social cues: priming

In some cases, it is not even necessary to wait the milliseconds necessary for the brain to pick up on the social cue, as they are served up on a plate. Imagine you are due to meet a senior representative of a wealth management firm for the first time. Just before her arrival, one of her colleagues leans towards you and says: "You'll like Sonya; she's a warm and friendly kind of person." Arguably, this statement doesn't contain much value. How can anyone possibly know whether you will like Sonya or

---

106 Chaudhry, S. J. and Lowenstein, G. (2016) 'Thanking, Apologizing, Bragging and Blaming: The Currency of Communication'. Working Paper. Department of Social and Decision Sciences, Carnegie Mellon University.

not? The colleague has no knowledge about your criteria for liking someone. He might not even share your definition of the word 'friendly'. Yet, the colleague was probably right – not because he had any special insight into your preferences, but simply because he said the words. By describing Sonya to you as warm and friendly, he increased the likelihood that you would perceive her in this way after the meeting. In this example, once the concept of 'friendly' is highlighted, our warmth detectors are effectively 'pre-activated', or 'primed'. So, even before the stimulus arrives, we actively search for cues that support our initial impression. This does not conjure up warmth out of nowhere, of course, it just makes any warmth-related cues that are present more salient and easily accessible to the cognitive system.[107]

Social cues: trust networks

The impact of warmth priming might have been even greater if you already trusted Sonya's colleague. In this configuration, trust becomes almost contagious. I trust a person; therefore, I tend to trust the people my trustee trusts. It is in this way that networks of connected individuals can emerge, all of whom trust each other implicitly. A trust network has the effect of reducing the risks for exchange partners. This is because the person who recommends a newcomer runs a risk of sanction by

---

107 Strack, F. and Martin, L. L. (1987) 'Thinking, judging, and communicating: A process account of context effects in attitude surveys'. In: Hippler, H. P., Schwarz, N. and Sudman, S. (eds.) *Cognitive Aspects of Survey Methodology*, Springer, New York.

other members of the network should the stranger prove to be untrustworthy.

MANUFACTURED TRUST

For a high-trust relationship to reliably emerge it should already be clear that it is the manager who must act to win the client's trust. And the bulk of these actions must take a form that does not involve the presentation of hard data like track records, relative performances, curriculum vitae, or investment case studies. This statement might rightly trouble some readers, as it smacks of manipulation. Indeed, all the push-back we have encountered from professionals in client-relationship management roles when we have discussed trust development has concerned the morality of any attempt by financial service providers to directly influence the trust-building process. An example of such a reaction is the following:

> "Aren't financial service providers doing their clients a disservice if they manufacture trust, even if it results in some advantages for those clients?"

These concerns deserve to be addressed.

The first and most important response to this is that one should always be honest with one's clients. It is both dangerous and counterproductive to feign characteristics that one does not genuinely possess to win business. Only truths withstand scrutiny and prevail over time. Given the goal is to build deep and lasting business relationships, an untruth would undermine those efforts. What we propose is simply to reveal truths that one might not previously have thought about revealing. The hesitancy might have been because:

- one thought it was unimportant

- one thought the client might not want to hear it

- one was unsure about the effect it might have.

For example, if I tell you that I have been married for 25 years and have four children – all of which is true – you might as a client perceive that I adhere to traditional values (alternatively, you might find me old-fashioned, or just plain old). You might perceive my abundance of children as evidence of my selflessness (or of my lack of discipline). The sharing of this information influences the way you perceive me. It might improve my perceived warmth and encourage a high-trust relationship between us (or not). To enable the client to perceive anything concerning my values or character, though, I must first share this seemingly unrelated piece of information.

The morality concerns are raised because trust-building targets the intuitive part of clients' selection decision. However, it also implies that service providers have an ethical alternative at their disposal. In building the foundations for interpersonal trust, there are some actions, like oxytocin diffusion or facial morphing, we have already labelled as unethical. In these cases, an ethical alternative is obvious: don't do it. However, most physical and social cues do not have ethical alternatives, because the absence of the cue is also a cue. Take the example of the colleague who describes a person as warm. It has the effect of influencing the perception of warmth, but so does every other possible conversation topic, including saying "Hello". Even if one refuses to engage the stranger in conversation, any ethical code would be still violated because silence is also a cue. So, as a rule, if there is an ethical alternative, take it, because integrity is essential to trust development over time. However, if the alternative to an intentional cue is to leave it to chance – with the risk that providence might unintentionally provoke mistrust – choose the trusting cue.

Finally, the trust built because of an action can never be described as 'manufactured', because that is the way trust is always built. It does not matter whether the actions that prompted the state of mind are deliberate or not. A flower is still genuine whether it is watered by a sprinkler or by rainfall. A flower needs water. It does not become a manufactured flower because the watering is intentional. The same applies to trust. Wherever it exists it has been initiated by someone sharing something with someone else – a sight, sound, word or gesture – that conveyed warmth. It does not work any other way. We merely propose not leaving this sharing to chance.

Clients need information to make judgements

The charge of manipulation could be levelled at any action that results in clients making choices they would not have made in the absence of the action, and the belief that the client could benefit from the action in no way lessens the charge. Yet trust-building actions should be about providing clients with *all* the information they need to make the right decision for them. Whether those clients are conscious of it or not, they want, need, and will actively seek information to make a judgement about service providers' intentions as well as about their competence. It is the service provider who stops short at competence data, and deliberately withholds information that would facilitate a client's intentions' judgement, who does a disservice.

SUMMARY

The adage, 'you only get one chance to make a first impression', is not strictly true, as the human brain will form an impression non-consciously during every encounter. However, that first encounter could either clear a path to interpersonal trust, or create an obstacle that must be undone during subsequent encounters. The above is far from being an exhaustive list of elements in the physical and social environment. The presence (or absence) of a scent, gesture, word, or even a heat source, could tip an individual towards the adoption of a trusting predisposition, or of a mistrusting one. This explains why interpersonal trust is such a volatile state. It also means that service providers must make every effort to shape the environment in a way that is advantageous for their message.

While actively seeking to influence the foundations of interpersonal trust, financial service providers must also be sensitive to the ethical boundaries of their actions. Where the moral thresholds are obvious – for instance, the introduction of an element into the physical or social environment that could never have existed naturally, like a morphed face or a synthesised hormone – such actions must be avoided. However, in most other cases, there is no cue-free alternative – the absence of a cue is also a cue. Human beings are even adept at identifying cues during a brief inspection of an unoccupied room. It is not unethical, therefore, to pay attention to every detail in the environment, from the serving of refreshments, to the fragrance of the hand cleansers in the washrooms. The role of warmth perceptions in social judgements is too important to be left to chance.

8 — THE CURSE OF COMPETENCE

To BE TRUSTED, a potential counterparty must be favourably perceived, not just on one of the two dimensions of social perception, but on both. Asset managers, as well as bankers, brokers, lawyers and other professionals in the financial services industry, sometimes struggle to be categorised as trustworthy. Although they are typically perceived as competent, people do not actually believe they have their clients' best interests at heart. On the contrary, people are convinced that bankers put bankers' interests first and clients' interests second. Bankers lack perceived warmth.

The lack of perceived warmth is particularly harmful for those in financial services because, in this industry, clients are exposed to risk. As warmth is the primary dimension of social perception, it always prompts an active response from clients. This is the evolutionary approach-avoidance dimension. Clients will actively seek out some managers, even though they have not achieved top-quintile performance, because they are warm. Clients will begrudgingly accommodate top-performing managers, even though they are cold but, as soon as performance slips, actively reject them. This means that warmth is not optional; it is essential. Yet, finance professionals are trained (and incentivised) to believe that competence is key. As a result, they use every interaction with clients to convey their competence, which is not only a missed opportunity, but also makes them appear colder. Competence can be a curse.

This chapter will reveal the trade-off that exists between warmth and competence perceptions. To be perceived as warm, service providers must be ready to sacrifice some of their perceived competence. This will not be welcome news for competence-focused professionals, but we will show that the trade-off is worth it, and suggest some methods to mitigate any loss of perceived competence.

TRUST IN BANKERS HITS NEW LOWS

By exposing the unscrupulous behaviour of some in the industry, the 2007/08 financial crisis worsened trust perceptions globally. An annual *Honesty and Ethics* poll by USA Today/ Gallup highlighted the deterioration of the perceived warmth of bankers.[108] In 2008, the public's perception of honesty and morality in the banking profession slumped to its lowest level since Gallup began the survey in 1977. Bankers were hardly popular before then either. As a testimony to the public's longstanding scepticism of this profession, one must only consider the enduring appeal of the literary classic, *Where Are the Customers'*

---

108 Gallup: www.gallup.com/poll/112264/nurses-shine-while-bankers-slump-ethics-ratings.aspx

Yachts? Or A Good Hard Look at Wall Street.[109] This scathing but light-hearted text, first published in 1940, exposed the underhanded techniques Wall Street bankers and brokers use to separate their customers from their money. Stock market indices rise and fall, fortunes are won and lost, but the bankers and brokers always come away wealthy. In the 1940s, too, it seems, this group was scorned because its members were the ones who could afford yachts, not their customers. It is conceivable that there is no period in history when moneylenders have been lauded for their benevolent intentions towards their clients.

FIGURE 8.1 – PROFESSIONALS IN THE FINANCIAL SERVICES INDUSTRY ARE PERCEIVED AS COMPETENT BUT COLD

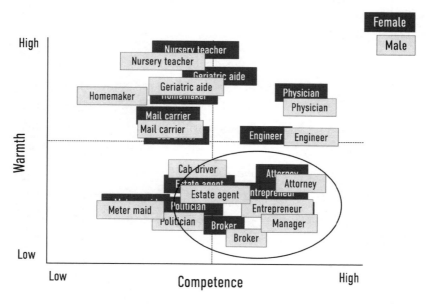

Source: Adapted from Imhoff, Woelki, Hanke and Dotsch (2013).

---

109 Schwed Jr., F. (2006) *Where Are The Customers' Yachts? or A Good Hard Look at Wall Street.* Wiley & Sons.

If bankers were never seen as warm, they were, at least up until the crisis, commonly perceived as capable. The chastened public might not have been surprised to hear accusations of collusion, exploitation or outright fraud levelled at the banking industry, as everybody already suspected these were unscrupulous people – clever, but unscrupulous. What surprised the public more in the wake of the crisis was to learn that some bankers and asset managers had absolutely no idea what they were getting into. So-called professionals were so ignorant of the riskiness of the products they bought, and of the unfolding financial calamity, some oversaw the bankruptcy of their own firms. The crisis, therefore, revealed them to be not only cold, but somewhat incompetent too. This explains why public sentiment turned so vociferously against the world of finance. In warmth-competence terms, passive accommodation turned to active harm.

A concerted effort began almost immediately after the crisis to repair the damaged perception of competence. Institutions, obviously keen to avoid their own financial ruin, began putting in place new oversight systems, and beefing up their controlling departments. Similarly, professional bodies in the finance industry sought to raise the skill levels of their members, to encourage the pursuit of recognised professional qualifications, and to bolster adherence to best practices of corporate governance. Governments across the world, too, have instructed their regulators to heap additional rules and constraints on financial institutions, all with the goal of ensuring there is no rerun of the crisis. Yet if financial professionals are to build trust with their clients, and improve their standing in the eyes of the public, they really needed to begin the task of improving their perceived warmth. This is what has been more significantly and durably lacking in the finance industry. Here, though, there has been no flurry of activity among professional bodies and regulators in recent years. Despite its importance for the establishment of trust, perceived warmth has been largely overlooked. This is the principal challenge for financial service providers. This is where institutions ought to concentrate their efforts.

THE WARMTH-COMPETENCE TRADE-OFF

It will not have escaped the attention of most readers that bankers and brokers are not the only professions to face hurdles in developing trust with their respective clients. In fact, people in most occupations attract ambivalent perceptions – they are commonly stereotyped as being low in one or other of the two key dimensions. Either they are rated as low in warmth and high in competence, or high in warmth and low in competence. In other words, they are largely corralled into a broad arc that sweeps from the top-left quadrant to lower-right quadrant. This suggests there might be a trade-off in these perceptions, and indeed there is: as soon as we perceive someone as warm, we become less likely to perceive him as competent, and vice versa. If asset managers and investment advisors want to be viewed as warm, there are two things they must be willing to do, both of which will likely oppose their instincts. The first is that they must stop pushing on the competence dimension. The second is that they must be ready to concede some of that competence perception in exchange for warmth.

FIGURE 8.2 – THE TRADE-OFF BETWEEN PERCEIVED WARMTH AND PERCEIVED COMPETENCE

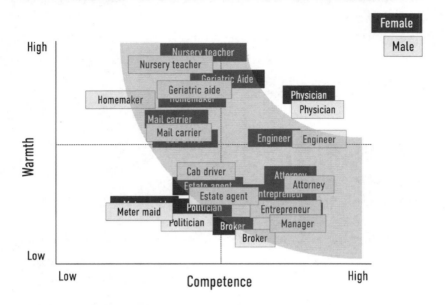

Source: Adapted from Imhoff, Woelki, Hanke and Dotsch (2013).

The prospect of either of these options will scare many finance professionals – not because they are beyond reach, but because they go against the grain. Being competent, and being seen to be competent, is a central part of their training. It is a characteristic they have likely cultivated over an entire professional career, and one to which they attach a considerable importance. The notion that one should be competent, but be shy about telling anyone about it, seems alien. Even more remote is the idea that one should choose to inform clients of one's lack of competence. The good news for these financial professionals is that they shouldn't worry too much about it.

A WORTHWHILE TRADE

To begin with, their clients attach more weight in their evaluations to the warmth perception than they do to the competence perception. As a result, the trade-off is well worth the effort – one additional unit of warmth, so to speak, will bring providers closer to a high-trust relationship than one additional unit of competence. Competence can be a curse rather than a blessing because it crowds out warmth. Another piece of good news is that they likely have plenty of competence perception to spare, as professionals in the finance industry are typically perceived as competent anyway. By the time the client has accepted the invitation to meet with representatives of an investment firm, the battle to convey competence has probably been won already. The representatives can afford to invest more effort in trying to convey warmth to the client than in trying to push competence perceptions even further. When the plan sponsor says, "Tell me about yourself", he is not asking for further demonstrations of competence – he is offering an opportunity to convey warmth. He wants to learn about good intentions.

STOP TRYING TO APPEAR COMPETENT

Asset managers' initial meetings with sponsors or investment consultants typically involve a sales pitch. Supported by a 'pitch book' of printed text, charts and tables, the fund management team will verbally present the firm, themselves, their decision-making process, their past performance, as well as a few carefully selected illustrations of successful past decisions. The pitch book and the verbal commentary will be very similar, if not identical, and they both will have one goal: to convince the potential clients of the asset managers' ability. Sales meetings are organised in this way because the asset management team quite reasonably believes that this is what clients want. Clients too believe that this is what they *ought to want*, because the managers' skill is what will determine the outcome of their mutual engagement. Yet those outcomes will also be influenced by the degree of trust in the relationship. So, whether the clients are conscious of it or not, they will also be searching for signs that such a relationship will be possible. Those signs are not found in the pitch book.

The pitch book is an essential, even legal, requirement. It is shown to others in the clients' organisation, and used to make initial comparisons with other asset management firms. Yet this is not the only thing that potential clients take back to the office with them. Their global impression of the management firm is only partially drawn in the pitch book. They will also take away their impression of the management representatives, even if they are unaware of the origins of these impressions. This information is shared internally too. The firm that has most effectively demonstrated its benevolent intentions will elicit positive sentiments among potential clients – confidence, hope, calm, liking. If the client's shortlist is composed of just two competing firms with comparable profiles, the warmth judgement will probably tip the balance.

Asset management teams that have two channels of communication at their disposal – verbal and written – should take advantage of at least one of them to provide clients with the information necessary to allow a judgement about the team's intentions. Rather than restate the lead manager's resumé, they should instead share the anecdote about the time he was almost ejected from the AGM of one of the companies in the portfolio after he loudly chastised the CEO for not adhering to the promises made the previous year. Such an anecdote reveals the manager's motivation to act in the client's interest.

Downplay one's status

Typically, observers associate high status with competence, and perceive high competence as lacking warmth. This means that it is counterproductive for asset managers to give themselves status in front of their clients. Rather, they should give their clients status. This, too, goes against the grain because many asset managers believe they are smarter than their clients, and probably a little nicer too. If one were to conduct a warmth-competence survey among asset managers, asking them to rate their clients, many perceptions would probably be ambivalent too. In the same way that clients' perception of asset managers influences their emotions and behaviours, so too will managers' perception of their clients.

A client perceived as warm, but not competent, will elicit pity from the manager. The consequence of this might be a sort of patronising paternalism. In the best case, the manager will try to be helpful and supportive, while at the same time talking down to the client. In the worst case, this ambivalent perception could result in unintentional neglect. For a client perceived as competent, but not warm, the elicited emotion is envy. The behavioural consequence here can be described as begrudged accommodation. In the best case, the manager will facilitate the relationship because of the potential advantages, but without enjoying it. This almost resentful association might also result from a fear the counterparty might use those 'smarts' to thwart the manager's goals. In the worst case, i.e. for the coldest clients, the manager might turn against them.

Imagine how useful it would be for the relationship if managers were to perceive all their clients as being in the top-right quadrant. It is possible. This is because we all have full control over the way we perceive others. All it requires is that we focus our attention in the right place. For example, even though one might rate someone as low on warmth (e.g. because he is obnoxious), there is invariably something about the person that we find nice (punctual, well-organised, remembers our names). If we focus our attention on the benchmark the person overshoots, our perception of that individual will improve. The same applies to a person who we consider to be not very smart. Here, too, some domain must exist where we consider him to be smart (knows the latest technology, speaks foreign languages). Again, if we focus our attention on the domain where the other excels, our perception of him will improve. This technique is known as *re-framing* the other – we mentally shift the axes of the four-quadrant graphic so that the other appears in the top right-hand corner. Managers must, therefore, learn to shift the focus of their attention, and do so actively. They must, for example, start the discussion in the domain where the other is smart (even if it leaves the manager looking less smart). Similarly, by focusing on the things that make the other person likeable, it becomes easier to see the world from his perspective. This is not about flattery; it is about adopting the mindset that prioritises the things clients obviously prioritise and, thereby, giving them status.

Shed the status symbols

Management firms should also remember that status is implied not simply by what they say but also by visible status symbols. If they put status symbols on display, it is tantamount to saying: "Look at me, I'm competent." A sales meeting, therefore, is not the place for asset managers to show off expensive watches behind monogrammed cuffs, or to talk about exclusive island getaways and luxury cars (or yachts). Such displays would cement their high status in the eyes of the client, and lift their perceived competence. However, status symbols also leave them looking colder.

CONCEDE COMPETENCE STRATEGICALLY

Admitting that one has made a mistake is rarely easy. Such concessions are particularly difficult when the client has been sold on the notion of competence. Yet the trade-off between warmth and competence means that the occasional admission of poor judgement can be advantageous. The client will not expect a competent individual or firm to be competent 100% of the time. So a periodic admission would not durably damage competence perceptions – but it *would* boost warmth perceptions.

A further piece of good news is that the concession of competence does not actually have to be in the same domain as the one where firms are trying to impress the client. A service provider can concede a lack of competence in any domain to accrue perceptions of warmth. For instance, I could say that I am a genius asset manager, but I'm hopeless at parallel parking; I can take good care of your portfolio, but do not let me near your houseplants. The admission that one is not competent in an unrelated domain doesn't detract from perceptions in the professional arena.

Competence judgements are about what outcomes a person can bring about. As we generally accept that people are more able in some activities than others, there is no contradiction if we perceive different levels of competence across a range of domains. In contrast, perceptions of warmth are about *why* someone wants to bring about an outcome. Is it for benevolent or malevolent reasons? This motivation, at least, should be broadly consistent irrespective of the activity. Someone judged to be a genuine friend in one domain cannot realistically emerge as an enemy in another without calling into question the initial judgement. For this reason, warmth perceptions tend to be transferable across domains.

We are only human

In one novel study, two groups of subjects were invited to watch a video of a very able, well-qualified job candidate being interviewed by a potential employer.[110] In reality, the interviewer

---

110 Helmreich, R., Aronson, E. and LeFan, J. (1970) 'To err is humanizing sometimes: Effects of self-esteem, competence, and a pratfall on interpersonal

and the interviewee were fictitious, with both roles played by professional actors. Both test audiences watched scenes that were identical in every regard except one: towards the end of the interview in one of the recordings, the interviewee accidentally spilled some coffee on his trousers. That was it. There was no other difference between the two scenes. There was, however, a significant difference in the audiences' evaluation of the candidates. The interviewee in the spilled-coffee video was rated as significantly warmer. He was judged not only as more suitable for the position than his more adroit alter-ego, but also the person the audience members said they would most like to work with. These favourable opinions resulted simply from his ham-fisted gesture with a coffee cup.

How are pratfalls related to warmth? One must not forget the egocentric stance. The talented, highly qualified job candidate does not really resemble most of us. He is distant and remote, almost superhuman. The blunder with the coffee cup had the effect of humanising him, making him resemble us more. We sometimes spill our beverages on our clothes; he spilled his coffee on his trousers; he is like us. In his moment of inattention, the job candidate revealed himself to be human, like the rest of us, and prone to making the occasional error. Given that we perceive ourselves as warm, well-suited to our professional positions, and agreeable to work with, we tend to perceive those who resemble us in the same favourable light. It should be noted, however, that embarrassing mistakes only improve warmth perceptions for exceptional candidates, the ones perceived as the most competent, as they are the ones who appear distant

attraction'. *Journal of Personality and Social Psychology*, 16 (2), 259–264.

and remote. A mediocre candidate does not suffer from this problem. A blunder committed by average candidates, therefore, only succeeds in making them appear below-average.

DETOUR: A PROMOTIONAL VIDEO

Notwithstanding the pratfall example above, a recorded video appears to be a convenient way to introduce a client to a firm, or to its key personnel, as it is a wholly scripted environment. Video producers can precisely determine the text, tone and appearance of the speaker. They can decide what appears in the background – furniture, pictures, plants, the (un)tidiness of the desk, etc. They also have some control over the focus of the viewers' attention. Admittedly, a video's rigidity denies its producers some opportunities to interact with the viewer and, therefore, to use all the possibilities for warmth projection. However, the director's camera can provide some opportunities that do not exist in a traditional business meeting. For instance, a camera perspective above the speaker's eye level gives height and status to the viewer, which is preferable to having the speaker 'looking down' on the viewer. The director also has the possibility to take the camera out of the meeting room and to introduce more dynamic backdrops, sounds and music. Critically, for many service providers, a scripted environment can spare them some of the fatal errors – inadvertent coldness – that can occur during a face-to-face encounter. Even in this case, though, producers must be sensitive to the foundations of interpersonal trust.

An asset manager video

During the research for this book the authors were invited to review a promotional video for a financial services firm. The star of the clip was a partner of the firm. He was first shown outside walking to the firm's building, then going up to his office. There were also several sequences with him leading an analysts' meeting. These shots were interspersed among the main video thread of him explaining his investment strategy to the viewer from the firm's conference room.

The first thing that must be said about the video is that its very existence is already an effort at conveying warmth. Clients like video clips. Many people would much prefer having a complex subject, like an investment strategy, explained to them via a video clip than via a written document. That the firm goes to the trouble and expense of producing a video demonstrates that it cares more about what the client hears than about what the firm says. This effort will not be lost on clients. However, this production missed several opportunities to convey warmth and stumbled into some coldness traps.

The principal character of the five-minute video delivered a flawless performance. One would expect a seasoned executive, sitting in the firm's conference room, to be able to explain the firm's investment strategy without getting confused or stumbling over his words. However, if one takes the camera outside into the street, this senior executive is just an ordinary pedestrian with little or no control over his environment. Yet in the promotional video no other pedestrian crosses his path. He doesn't dodge a collision with a jogger while turning a corner, or hesitate before entering the revolving door. He doesn't have to run to get out of the rain. These are the kinds of things that happen to ordinary people when we go outside. For him to misstep in such in environment would not have taken away from his abilities as an asset manager, but it would have given viewers an early opportunity to see him as human, as one of us.

Between entering the building and sitting down at his desk, the partner doesn't interact with any other staff member. There are no smiles, greetings or handshakes. This might demonstrate dedication and urgency to his work, but it makes him appear cold and unfriendly. There is some evidence emerging to suggest that people who brag and blame are perceived as colder but more competent, whereas those who thank and apologise are perceived as warmer but less competent.[111] Had the partner been filmed mouthing a 'thank you' to a colleague while, perhaps, collecting some documents from his desk, a warmth perception might have been encouraged.

The analysts' meeting takes place in a wood-panelled boardroom, furnished with leather-upholstered chairs. The partner sits at the head of a long table. He is obviously the boss, and the team members' attention and communication is directed toward him. The scene gives the partner, and the firm, importance and status. Similarly, many camera angles are from a perspective below his eye-level – one even looks up at him from the floor. Again, status is conferred to the partner, not to the viewer. The consequence is that the partner will be perceived as competent – but it becomes less likely that viewers will perceive him as warm.

---

111 Chaudhry, S. J. and Loewenstein, G. (2016) 'Thanking, Apologizing, Bragging and Blaming: The Currency of Communication'. Working Paper. Department of Social and Decision Sciences, Carnegie Mellon University.

SUMMARY

Financial services often involve sizeable risks for clients, which means that trust is essential for many engagements. This trust requires that the provider be evaluated positively on both the warmth and competence dimensions. This is not the only industry where customers are faced with risks, of course. Parents run a risk when they entrust their toddlers to a nursery school teacher; patients run a risk when they agree to go under a surgeon's knife. However, recognising that they are already perceived by parents as warm, nursery school teachers make a conscious effort to appear competent, for example, by focusing on their contribution to the child's development and learning. Surgeons, recognising that they are already perceived as competent, deliberately focus on their bedside manner. Financial services professionals, in contrast, have seemingly not yet recognised that their missing 'it' is warmth.

Asset managers and financial advisors, either as a product of their training, or of the recruitment or reward policies of their employers, tend to attach a great deal of importance to appearing competent – and little to appearing warm. In communication with their clients, for instance, they dedicate much, if not all the bandwidth, to conveying this one-sided impression of themselves. Sadly, no amount of competence can compensate for a lack of warmth. Furthermore, as warmth is the primary dimension of social perception and always provokes an active response, the client's overall impression will not be positive unless he perceives the provider as warm.

As there is often a trade-off between perceived warmth and perceived competence, financial service providers must do two things that might strike many as unfamiliar, if not unnatural: they must stop pushing on the competence dimension; and, they must be prepared to sacrifice their competence – in the perception of their clients – in exchange for warmth.

9 – DEVELOPING INTERPERSONAL TRUST

T HE SEEDS OF trust might be sown in the first moments of an encounter, but a seed is still seed, not a full-grown plant. As already described in a previous chapter, the physical and social cues in the environment do not create trust. They merely encourage associations in the mind that make the psychological state of trust more accessible. Nonetheless, they are important because they can either smooth the path to trust or impede it. If those associations are positive for trust, we will more easily recognise subsequent elements that confirm this initial impression. We will also tend to give any ambiguities the benefit of the doubt. If, on the other hand, those associations are negative for trust, we will more readily recognise any information that confirms the other's untrustworthiness, and treat ambiguities sceptically.

Even if the seed of trust falls on fertile soil, then, it still needs water, sunlight and nutrients to grow. This chapter will focus on the key ingredients one must bring to a relationship to encourage the development of trust over time. We will also discuss what one must do if, despite all of one's efforts, the trust relationship suffers a setback. How does one go about repairing a loss of trust? We begin, though, with the key ingredients, which must be present over the life of the trust relationship. They can be regrouped into four broad categories:

- value congruence

- caring

- vulnerability

- psychological distance.

VALUE CONGRUENCE

In the simplest terms, value congruence means that the trustee adheres to a set of values the trustor finds acceptable. In the context of a business relationship, examples of values clients might approve of in their service providers could include things like fairness, honesty or openness. Often, these will be the same set of values clients themselves adhere to. Such shared values signal that the counterparty is 'one of us', and that benevolent intentions are to be expected. However, clients might also find acceptable the values espoused by some idealised norm, or cultural default, even if adherence to those values is out of the clients' reach. For instance, clients might find 'reliability' or 'good manners' to be highly desirable values for a business partner to adhere to, even if those clients struggle to be reliable or good-mannered themselves.

Although the values mentioned so far are honourable, value congruence does not make moral judgements. What is important for trust is the sharing of values, not their ethics. This means that two individuals with nefarious ambitions can nonetheless trust each other because immoral values can also be shared. Strong bonds of trust emerge, therefore, just as commonly among fraudsters and terrorists as among business partners. Indeed, trust might develop more easily among the former because the shared values are more obvious, and because the parties have no legal recourse in case the other reneges on a deal. Business partners, in contrast, might not recognise their shared values at once, nor be motivated to search for them.

The list of acceptable values is not limited solely to business-relevant characteristics. Any values the counterparties share, or that reflect those of some perceived ideal, will also be acceptable. A firm's long history in the investment management industry, its independence, or its patronage, could be among those values. Its support for charities, defence of the environment, sponsorship of sports or the arts, or even its political leanings, all represent potential values. Its Scottish-ness might be an acceptable value, even if clients are not Scottish, or precisely because they are. Even the age, education and religion of the firm's representatives could appear on the list of acceptable values. So, to develop trust, it is important, firstly, to know which values clients find acceptable and, secondly, to use them as a foundation for client communication.

Communication

Persuasion can be more effective if one's arguments are grounded in the values held by one's audience.[112] In US politics,

---

112 Feinberg, M. and Willer, R. (2015) 'From Gulf to Bridge: When Do Moral Arguments Facilitate Political Influence?' *Personality and Social Psychology*

for example, observers have noted that the most strongly held political views are grounded in moral values, which partisans of each group see as universal and absolute. In surveys, researchers have highlighted, for example, that liberals tend to endorse moral values centred on benevolence, social justice, equality, fairness and reciprocity more strongly than conservatives. In contrast, conservatives attach more importance to in-group loyalty, authority, patriotism, traditionalism and sanctity than liberals.[113] These values are the starting point for each group's intuitions and attitudes, which means that liberals and conservatives struggle to convince each other of their respective political positions.

This mutual incomprehension caused by value incongruence is especially marked when morally-charged issues – like same-sex marriage, universal healthcare, global warming or military spending – are up for discussion. In experiments, scientists found that liberals tasked to convince conservatives (and vice versa) of their respective political position would, by default, frame their arguments in terms of their own values rather than those of their political opponents. This tended to reduce the effectiveness of their message. When arguments appealed to the values of the audience, however, they were more persuasive. It is counterintuitive to frame one's arguments in terms of values one does not endorse, which is why political discussions can be so polarised, and why political opponents have such difficulty finding compromise. Business partners, however, needn't have

Bulletin. l 41 (12), 1665–1681. doi: 10.1177/0146167215607842.

113 Graham, J., Haidt, J., Nosek, B. A. (2009) 'Liberals and conservatives rely on different sets of moral foundations'. *Journal of Personality and Social Psychology*, 96, 1029–1046. doi: 10.1037/a0015141.

this problem. They must only identify the values they share with their counterparties and use these as the foundations for their arguments.

Know your customer

'Know your customer' is the label given to a regulatory requirement imposed on banks, accountants, lawyers and other service providers in the financial industry, to verify the identity of their counterparties. Its goal is to prevent these agents from becoming unwitting accomplices to money laundering and other illicit activities. The rules call for enhanced due diligence to determine the customer's identity and affiliations. However, none of these recommendations encourage firms to actively discover their clients' values. This is a shame, as this pursuit might allow them to develop closer trust relationships.

The most obvious starting point in the search for clients' values is the annual report, where at least stated values, sponsorships and style preferences are on full display. Websites and advertising also provide clues to values. A review of a client's other counterparties could also reveal some unifying characteristics that reflect their shared values. Failing the availability of public sources of information, service providers could simply ask senior individuals or norm-setters in the client's firm what their values are. In principal, this appears to be the most straightforward option. Yet people sometimes struggle to recognise what their organisation's values are and, even if they do, have difficulty in effectively articulating them.

Once trustors' values have been identified, trustees must search among their own values to see where there is an overlap. Here, again, we must caution against feigning values that one does not genuinely hold. Such pretence is unlikely to survive the tests of scrutiny or of time. Furthermore, once the deceit is discovered, it would undermine the client's perception of warmth – the most important dimension in the development of trust. Feigning values is also unnecessary: the list of values two partners could possibly share is so long, it is almost inconceivable that there is no overlap. The overlap will not be the same for each client, which creates a daunting management task for client relationship professionals. This is especially the case if management responsibilities are subdivided according to client size, type or geographical location, as is often the case. In this respect, a more effective subdivision might be according to client values.

Having found genuine value congruence, trustors must make sure the trustees are aware of it. This task must be handled delicately because a value is not a value if one needs to tell people about it. Reliable people do not have to remind others of their reliability; honest folk do not have to say that they are honest. If they do, it raises suspicion among their audiences that the opposite might be true. So, shared values need to be put on display discreetly, such that trustors find them on their own. For service providers, this discreet 'value placement' includes everything from types of events one chooses to sponsor or attend, to the artwork on display in reception.

CARING

A caregiver is someone who pays anxious attention to another's well-being. Parents, for instance, care for their offspring. They protect them from danger, imminent or potential. They prepare them for the future that awaits them by imparting life skills and formal education. They also take time to communicate with them, at the speed and comprehension level of the child, not of the parent. This is the way that caring should be interpreted in the business context, too.

How do businesses care?

Service providers who care for their clients worry about their clients' well-being in the widest sense. They are considerate about their clients' business objectives, but also express concern for anything, present or future, that could affect their broader objectives. Caring service providers seek to educate their clients and, crucially, take time to do so. The provision of education, training or technical assistance to a business partner has a dual effect here: it showcases the service provider's competence, and it demonstrates an interest in the partner's wider success. If this education is not fully paid for, it also makes the service provider vulnerable to opportunism on the part of the client. This vulnerability, as we shall see below, can also contribute to trust development.[114] Finally, caring businesses share any information they have that could further their clients' objectives, whether

---

114 Sako, M. (1998) 'Does trust improve business performance?' in Lane, C. and Bachmann, R. (eds.). *Trust within and between organizations: Conceptual issues and empirical application*, (pp.88–117). Oxford: Oxford University Press.

that information is directly relevant to the business engagement or not. This kind of behaviour reveals that they are more interested in the clients' outcomes than they are about selling more products, or taking a client from a competitor. Caring demonstrates to clients that they occupy a privileged position, that they are part of the in-group, that they are 'one of us'. It therefore implies benevolent intentions and typically prompts reciprocation.

One very powerful caring signal an asset management firm can send to its clients is a decision to close a fund to new investors or, at least, to signal it will do so once a specified asset level is reached. Investment funds commonly experience diminishing returns as they become larger. This is partly because larger funds are less nimble. Their sheer size means that any buying or selling they do could impact the market price for the target security in an unfavourable direction, thereby worsening the portfolio returns. Large funds also face a shrinking pool of investible assets. It becomes impossible to outperform the market if the fund has grown to the point that it resembles the market. Hence, allowing assets under management to reach a size where investment outcomes are likely to be worsened is not in the interests of the client. However, large funds are very much in the interests of the management firm, as it charges fees as a function of its asset base. If the fund stops accumulating assets even though marginal revenues from those additional assets are above the marginal costs of servicing them, the firm is foregoing profits. A management team that chooses to close a fund to new investors demonstrates clearly that it puts clients' interests ahead of its own.

A not-so-random act of kindness

Just outside your office building there is some unevenness in the paving stones that some pedestrians overlook. You have been tripped up there once before. You have also witnessed countless people stumble, and even fall, at the same spot. The paving is scheduled for repair. Today, however, you have agreed to greet a new client in front of the building. As he arrives you notice that his trajectory will take him precisely over the spot where the paving stones are uneven. "Watch your step there," you warn, "the paving stones are little uneven." As a result of your intervention, your guest steps over the unevenness and arrives without stumbling or falling. The client appreciates the warning and, non-consciously, perceives you as warmer. This perception positively affects the trust relationship between you. What is wrong with that?

Some might argue that it depends on your motivation for issuing the warning. If your sole reason for cautioning the client was to benefit from the improved warmth perception, and thereby win trust, the warning was insincere at best, dishonest at worst. This line of reasoning, however, implies that you were indifferent to the client's outcome. This is almost certainly not the case. Irrespective of your knowledge of trust development, you would probably not have wanted your guest to fall flat on his face. The gesture was, in this case, sincere. It also resulted in a genuine gain for the client, i.e. not stumbling or falling. The client wants to be warned whenever there are uneven paving stones, hence you acted in the way the client prefers, even demands.

The opportunities to act in a way that promotes a client's broader interests are usually not as obvious as an uneven paving stone. An intense focus on the narrow interests of the business relationship often obscures important events that might be unfolding elsewhere. In addition, the trust relationship might not yet have developed to a point where the client feels comfortable revealing the nature of these broader interests. Periodically, therefore, one must take a step back and consider one's clients from a wider perspective. For example, given their statements, recent actions, emerging competitive or regulatory pressures, what are their likely goals? What can one do (if anything at all) to help in that pursuit? What resources does one have at one's disposal – information, ideas, time, skills, connections, etc., that one could deploy to further clients' interests? These resources do not have to be deployed at zero cost, of course. Caring is not about giving stuff away for free – it is about adopting the anxious mindset of a caregiver.

VULNERABILITY

The more a client is exposed to risk, the more important trust becomes in a business relationship. Allowing oneself to be vulnerable to someone else is an expression of trust. It is a recognition that one believes the other has benevolent intentions, and will not exploit that vulnerability. This is true for the client, but also for the service provider. Although service providers cannot determine the degree of a client's risk, they can set the level of their own vulnerability. If they make themselves vulnerable to their clients – i.e. put themselves in a position where clients could exploit them, if they were so minded – clients would recognise this as an expression of trust. The desire to reciprocate this warm gesture encourages clients to validate the trust that was implied in the gesture.

At the top of chapter 7, we recounted the tale of Henry and the stockbroker. In it, the broker seemed able to win Henry's trust in the space of a short taxi ride, without mentioning stocks or stockbroking. One of the contributing factors to this outcome was his vulnerability. Right at the outset of the relationship, the stockbroker revealed some personal information about himself. The news that the man's ten-year old considered his father to be "a loser" was hardly a damning indictment. Yet it was certainly not something he would want everyone to know about. This was a piece of personal information that could only be shared discreetly, in the back of a cab, with someone he trusted. Had Henry's intentions been wicked, he could have embarrassed the broker by spreading this information widely. He could also have shared the latter's dislike of the tie he had received as a birthday present, and the fact that he stashed it in his pocket at the first opportunity. The broker is aware of this, and yet he exposed himself to the risk. In so doing, he signalled to Henry that he trusted him. Henry reciprocated trust with trust.

Reciprocation

In the trust exchange, it is advantageous to be a first mover. A precipitous act of trust by one party to another is not only difficult to ignore, but also difficult to treat as being motivated by anything other than trust. Such gestures are, therefore, able to overcome a counterparty's natural inclination to be defensive, and accelerate trust development.[115] In one study

---

115 Weber, M. J., Malhotra, D. and Murnighan, J. K. (2000) 'Normal Acts of Irrational Trust: Motivated Attributions and the Trust Development Process'. In *Research in Organizational Behavior*. Vol. 22, edited by B. Staw and R. Sutton,

of interorganisational alliances, in which the failure rate was as high as 80%, researchers discovered that one of the best predictors of success was a large, unilateral commitment by one of the parties ahead of the investment by the other.[116] Examples of such commitments included promises of exclusivity; sharing proprietary information; internal reorganisation; and the signing of long-term supply contracts with third-parties. The size and risk of the commitments signalled the party's sincerity and created a context in which reciprocity was expected. In no case, noted the authors, did any counterparty abuse the unilateral gesture; in every case, the partner responded by cooperating.

The impact of contracts on trust

John Paul Getty held an opinion of contracts to which numerous scholars have subscribed: "If you can trust someone, you don't need a contract. If you can't trust him, a contract is useless."[117] This view implies that contractual agreements do not foster trust. It might even be that the very existence of a formal contract 'crowds out' the emergence of trust.[118] This might be true in many informal situations, where the sudden appearance of a written contract could be seen as a snub, and disrupt what

---

75–101. Elsevier Science.

116 Gulati, R., Khanna, T. and Nohria, N. (1994) 'Unilateral Commitments and the Importance of Process in Alliances'. *MIT Sloan Management Review*, 35 (3), 61–69.

117 Malhotra, D., and Murnighan, J. K. (2002) 'The effects of contracts on interpersonal trust'. *Administrative Science Quarterly*, 47, 534–559.

118 Shapiro, S. (1987) 'The Social Control of Impersonal Trust'. *American Journal of Sociology*, 93 (3), 623–658.

might otherwise have been an upward trust spiral. However, in the financial services industry, relationships between providers and their clients invariably take place within a legal framework where contracts are the norm. The impact on trust from contracts comes from their content rather than their existence.

Although contracts are typically signed only after the selection decision has been made, model contracts are available much earlier in the process. Providers who insist on unconventional contractual conditions will also tend to flag them to potential clients early in the process. This means that the terms of legal agreements will also figure in clients' perceptions of warmth and competence. We recognise that many financial service providers will be powerless to influence the contents of their client contracts in any significant fashion. However, it is nonetheless worthwhile to briefly dwell on the impact these can have on trust building.

The principal trust-building mechanism at work in contracts is again reciprocation. Do the contractual terms imply that clients can be trusted, or do they anticipate some unscrupulousness on their part? If clients recognise an expression of trust in the contract, they are more likely to reciprocate it with gestures of trust of their own. If, on the other hand, the contract reflects suspicion and hesitation on the part of the service provider, clients are more likely to return the same in kind.

Contractual control and coordination

Contracts can be categorised as having, primarily, one of two functions – control or coordination.[119] The controlling clauses in a contract focus on the rights and obligations of the parties. They are typically rigid and binding, are filled with detailed specifications, provide for performance monitoring, and set out strict sanctions for non-compliance. Coordinating clauses set out the framework for achieving mutual objectives. They focus on the resources to be deployed, schedules and intermediate goals, lines of communication and feedback, methods for conflict resolution, and contingency plans.

Contractual controlling might reflect legal diligence and thoroughness and thereby convey competence. However, such controlling contracts also send the message that the counterparty cannot be trusted. They imply that opportunism or other deviant behaviour is feared, or even expected. In response to such clauses, the counterparty might seek to exploit any unattended legal loopholes, treat activity that is not expressly forbidden as permissible by implication, or even sabotage the surveillance mechanism.[120] This kind of behaviour would prompt the service provider to step up performance monitoring, thereby confirming the distrustful initial beliefs of both counterparties, and breeding further resentment. Even incentives to cooperation, such as performance bonuses, are in fact controlling mechanisms that could have a negative impact

---

119 Lumineau, F. (2014) 'How Contracts Influence Trust and Distrust'. *Journal of Management.* 43 (5), 1553–1577.

120 Kramer, R. M. (1999) 'Trust and distrust in organizations: Emerging perspectives, enduring questions'. *Annual Review of Psychology*, 50, 569–598.

on trust. The presence of an additional economic incentive also sends the message that the counterparty might not be motivated to cooperate without it.

In contractual coordination, the focus on shared goals emphasises value congruence. Similarly, the establishment of lines of communication encourages information sharing. The inherent flexibility of such contracts, though, leaves the service provider vulnerable to opportunism, most commonly in the ease with which counterparties can escape the contract, and in the latitude it allows them to act in ways which violate the spirit of the agreement. Hence, firms who try to express warmth through trusting contracts will occasionally encounter betrayal. However, the implied message in this vulnerability is that the counterparty is trusted, and that cooperation is anticipated. Our human tendency to reciprocate trust with trust leads to a virtuous cycle of cooperation without the need for additional economic incentives. And even former betrayers sometimes return as trustworthy counterparties because people simply prefer to be trusted.

Informal contracts

We concede that individuals within a firm will not have much influence over formal contracts with clients. However, there is typically freedom to set up informal contracts between individuals in each organisation that deal with the mode and motivation for cooperation. These informal contracts supplement the formal ones. They verbalise the shared values between the two parties, make explicit their mutual objectives and how these are to be measured, and set out a mechanism for the early resolution of conflicts. Such informal contracts can be sealed with a simple handshake. They communicate trust at an individual level, even if the signal is missing at an institutional level.

PSYCHOLOGICAL DISTANCE AND TRUST

The language of trust is rich with physical metaphors. For example, we speak about an outcome that is predictable as *foreseeable*, describe an event that is unlikely as *remote*, and depict a person we trust as *close*. The reason we often relate that which is trustworthy to that which is physically close – i.e. in reach of our senses – might be because they share some important characteristics. Nearby objects are tangible, reliable and unambiguous; the same applies to people we find trustworthy. We believe we know them, and know their intentions, which we assume to be good. They are predictable and dependable. These people do not need to be physically close to be trusted, although it helps – e.g. consider a bricks-and-mortar store vs an online store. But they need to be perceived to be close; they need to be psychologically close.

Physically close objects and outcomes can be experienced directly through our senses because they are here and now. Yet we can easily imagine things that are happening somewhere else or to someone else. We can envisage outcomes that will occur in the distant future, as well as those that *might have occurred* had history taken a different path. Yet we do not experience those other outcomes directly. Instead, we construct a mental representation of the outcome. Our 'experience' is still real, in the sense that it evokes genuine emotions and actions. We make plans and decisions based on mental constructions in the same way that we would on information gathered with our own senses. Yet, a mental representation involves a degree of abstraction. The starting point for these mental constructions is always the self, anchored in the present. Thinking that takes us away from the 'here and now' – and, critically, from the 'me' – becomes metaphorically 'distant', 'remote', even 'alien'. Hence, reducing psychological distance becomes a key goal in efforts to develop trust.[121]

Psychological distance comprises four main dimensions: time, space, social and hypothetical distance. If we consider something that will occur in the distant future, or that happened in the distant past (temporal distance), it becomes more abstract, less detailed. The same applies if we must envisage things that are in a different place, e.g. in another building, city or country (spatial distance). Abstraction is also required if we try to envision circumstances from an unknown person's perspective, compared to from our own or from a familiar person's (social distance), or if we try to imagine events that are merely probable or counterfactual (hypothetical distance). As we move along these psychological dimensions, our thinking changes in systematic ways. When a mental representation is distant, we focus on its abstract, general properties. Imagine the release of the latest iteration of a popular smartphone is announced for one year's time. We will think about its overall desirability, and how it might

---

121 Darke, P. R., Brady, M. K., Benedicktus, R. L., and Wilson, A. E. (2016) 'Feeling close from afar: The role of psychological distance in offsetting distrust in unfamiliar online retailers'. *Journal of Retailing*, 92, 287–299.

compare to earlier models or those of other manufacturers. We are in the 'why?' frame of mind. "Why should I buy it?" As the mental representation becomes closer – it is here and now – we focus instead on its concrete, specific details. Now we think about when our contracts are up for renewal, or whether we can afford it. We are in the 'how?' frame of mind. "How can I buy it?" Clients who are in the 'why?' mode need proximity and warmth; clients in the 'how?' mode can be shown competence.

The various dimensions of psychological distance are interrelated. This means that if an object moves towards our 'mental horizon' on one dimension, research suggests, it moves on all of them simultaneously.[122] We perceive, therefore, outcomes that lie in the far future (greater time distance) as also being less probable (greater hypothetical distance). We perceive things that are improbable (greater hypothetical distance) as more likely to occur to unknown others (greater social distance), and somewhere else (greater spatial distance).

Psychological distance also works in both directions, namely that objects and outcomes described in abstract terms are perceived to be distant. Hence the description 'financial advisor' is distant. 'A financial advisor who enjoys sports' is closer. 'A financial advisor who broke his little finger while playing tennis' is closer still. A successful asset manager is distant, but one 'whose thoroughness in analysing balance sheets has helped to sidestep many unrewarded risks' is closer. The level of detail implies proximity, which reduces psychological distance, and so might lower the hurdle to interpersonal trust. This is the reason firms

---

122 Stephan, E., Liberman, N. and Trope, Y. (2000) 'Politeness and social distance: A construal level perspective'. *Journal of Personality and Social Psychology*, 98, 268–280.

seek endorsements from celebrities or from social media stars. Consumers perceive them as close because they have concrete knowledge of them, or because they resemble them.

Investment returns are only probable and lie in the distant future. So, although talking about them is unavoidable, the discussion will not shrink psychological distance. Yet some elements of the investment manager's service are both certain and immediate. So service providers must also talk to clients about the things they can guarantee (and stick to their promises), and do so in concrete terms. Hence, rather than saying 'we are supportive of our clients', one should be specific: 'we help our clients with concrete X'. Finally, in any communication, one must make it as easy to understand as possible. Service providers must try to adopt the perspective of their clients and, thereby, reduce the client's need to see a situation from another's perspective. They should also ensure that any communication is comprehensible, and that written material is easy to read. Even a poorly chosen font has been shown to increase psychological distance.[123]

---

123 Alter, A. L., and Oppenheimer, D.M. (2008) 'Effects of Fluency on Psychological Distance and Mental Construal (or Why New York Is a Large City, but New York Is a Civilized Jungle)'. *Psychological Science.* 19 (2), 161–167. doi: 10.1111/j.1467-9280.2008.02062.x.

TRUST REPAIR

An oft-repeated adage goes: 'Trust takes years to build but can be destroyed in seconds.' As variations of it exist in texts going back some 70 years,[124] it came as a surprise not to find any scientific evidence to support its two principal contentions. On the contrary, the evidence presented here illustrates that trust is not even something to be built and destroyed. Trust is *two* things to be built and destroyed – warmth and competence.

Which trust have you lost?

Competence-based trust does indeed take years to build. This kind of trust is based on hard data and lengthy observation. One observes that a counterparty has the means – ability, resources, contacts, etc. – necessary to bring about an outcome. One therefore concludes that he is competent. Then something occurs that conflicts with this conclusion – a poor outcome. Although the outcome is disappointing, this setback is unlikely to cause us to call into question our earlier judgement about the counterparty's competence. The means are sometimes insufficient to secure every desired outcome. In short, one does not expect competent people to be competent all the time.[125] If, however, another unsatisfactory outcome follows, and then another, one might begin to suspect that the counterparty is not

---

124 Quote: "Good will takes years to build and seconds to destroy" in *The Bankers Monthly* – Volume 65, p.40. Hanover Publishers, 1948.

125 Cuddy, A. J. C., Glick, P. and Beninger, A. (2011) 'The dynamics of warmth and competence judgments, and their outcomes in organizations'. *Research in Organizational Behavior*, 31, 73–98.

competent after all. Competence-based trust, therefore, takes a long time to build, but also takes a long time to destroy.

Warmth-based trust, as we have seen, could emerge in an instant. Right from the very first encounter, one can decide that a counterparty's motivation to bring about an outcome is in one's best interests. If, subsequently, that counterparty displays any behaviour that indicates that he is in fact pursuing his own selfish interests, that earlier judgement is completely overturned. If somebody is 'on our side', we expect them to be there all the time, and under all circumstances. Warmth-based trust, indeed, takes seconds to destroy, but it only takes seconds to build.

One of the reasons warmth-based trust is so much more fragile than competence-based trust is the ease with which warmth can be faked. Trustors know that trustees have an interest to appear both competent and warm. As competence is difficult to feign if one does not have it, trustors can be reasonably satisfied that their judgements are valid. Indeed, the longer the period of observation, the more they can be convinced of the validity of their judgement. In contrast, people can pretend to be warm, even over long periods of time. Consequently, trustors know they must be particularly vigilant, even sceptical, because their judgements might not be valid. Hence, any indication that warmth might not be genuine can expect to be heavily sanctioned. This difference explains the emotions trustors experience following a loss of trust. As a rule, if the emotion experienced after a setback is *disappointment,* then it is most likely that competence-based trust was lost. *Betrayal* is the emotion most closely associated with a loss of warmth-based trust. This distinction is important for service providers to make if they want to repair a trust relationship.

Regaining competence-based trust primarily involves providing new observations that confirm the original judgement, i.e. delivering more satisfactory outcomes. Sometimes this might require enhancing one's abilities, securing additional resources, or developing wider contacts, in order to make such outcomes more likely. However, the relationship can survive the poor result. Furthermore, those service providers who have also earned a reserve of warmth-based trust will find their clients more indulgent of the occasional competence-related setback.

The task of repairing warmth-based trust is far more daunting. It is conceivable that it can never be repaired because the client might view subsequent efforts to convey warmth cynically. While the relationship might survive based on competence alone, it might become more formal and distanced. It will also become more fragile because it is less resistant to any competence-related setback. Therefore, the repair of warmth-based trust will often begin by removing the person (or persons) responsible for the betrayal, and a public mea culpa.

SUMMARY

Efforts to build trusting business relationships must be maintained over the life of the relationship. As client perceptions of their service provider are refined and revised with each successive interaction, each one is an opportunity to promote trust. We have regrouped into four categories the targets for action:

- value congruence
- caring

- vulnerability

- psychological distance.

The desired result of efforts on all these fronts is to make clients feel as though they are cherished members of our family. Our family members are 'close' and trusted. We share the same values, attitudes and perspectives, and so we are easier to understand and to predict. We care for our families, not just on a transactional basis, but in the widest possible sense. We deploy resources to help them and are watchful over them. We are comfortable being vulnerable towards them, and are respectful when they do the same. These goals rely vastly more on service providers' warmth than on their competence. That warmth is also more fragile, and difficult to repair, if ever it is lost.

10 — THE MISSING 'IT'

T HE PERCEPTION THAT it put its clients' best interests ahead of its own, might have been the elusive characteristic that allowed *ABC Investment Management* – the competitor firm in our introductory chapter – to be held up as a benchmark by clients in a sales meeting with another firm. Similarly, the subtle trait that enabled *XYZ Asset Management* to win mandates despite, as it was claimed, its inferior products, could have been the values it shared with its clients, as shared values signal benevolent intentions. The missing 'it' lies in the trust relationship between these firms and their clients. More specifically, as clients typically perceive financial service providers as competent, the missing 'it', for them, is actually just warmth.

The same reasoning helps to explain why the gourmet burger restaurant, and the consulting surgeon, struggle to get their messages across: in the eyes of their 'clients', they lack warmth, and are psychologically distant. In both cases, their clients probably suspect they are competent and that the quality of their products and services is superior to that which is available across the street. Yet because there is risk, they need to know them, and to know their intentions and values. They need them to be closer, and to be concrete instead of abstract. In short, they need to trust them before entering into an exchange.

For a restaurant diner, the burger chain is more familiar, so psychologically closer. As such, it is perceived as more trustworthy, and a meal there is perceived as less risky. This judgement is particularly pertinent if the diner is new in the city, but knows the burger chain from his hometown. To convey warmth, the gourmet restaurant must get closer to the client. The restaurant must be given a face, perhaps that of the owner, and a name. This makes it more concrete and specific. Its products must also move closer, for example, by promoting its use of regional products from local suppliers. These products might be ugly, tasteless and of little nutritional value. Indeed, they might be objectively inferior in every possible respect – but their proximity makes them appear more trustworthy, and so less risky.

The surgeon's insistence on the use of statistics, league tables and empirical data to inform the patient supports the perception of competence but worsens the perception of warmth. He too should seek to get closer to the patient. The closest psychological distance is that of a family member. "If you were my son/mother/spouse, I would recommend…" The surgeon should also discuss the implications of the surgery, not just in terms of the immediate medical consequences but in terms of the patient's broader goals. What will the surgery mean for his participation in family activities, in the local choir, or in an upcoming marathon? Only once the patient is convinced the surgeon has his best interests at heart, will trust emerge, and the operation appear less risky.

Warmth has been neglected in the financial services sector for a long time. The common belief was not only that competence was the characteristic that mattered, but also that superior performance – i.e. a demonstration of competence – could compensate for any misgivings a client might have:

'Why should I have to show that I put clients' interests first? Can't they see that I invest my own money in my fund?'

'Why do I need to share clients' values? My superior returns allow them to pursue more of their values than they would be able to with the mediocre returns of my competitors.'

Unfortunately, for the emergence and development of trust, the perception of competence only brings service providers so far. The primary dimension of interpersonal trust is the perception of warmth. Without it, many service providers might not even earn the opportunity to demonstrate their competence. Furthermore, there are no regulatory restrictions to conveying warmth and to building trust with clients. As long as one is honest and ethical about what one shares with clients, regulators are unlikely to caution service providers about being *excessively warm*. This means that warmth remains a terrain where firms can still express a competitive advantage.

Prior to embarking on this quest for the missing 'it', we could only intuit where the journey would lead. In the meantime, we recognise that we use the described mechanisms in our judgements about others constantly. We judge salespeople at the store, presenters on TV, teachers at the kids' schools and, especially, electoral candidates, in terms of warmth and competence or as near or far. As one becomes more conscious of these perceptions, one also sees increasing opportunities to alter them. We certainly hope this is the case for our readers, too, because the need to perceive trustworthiness in financial service providers, and to be involved in trusting business relationships, is growing.

The post-crisis era of low yields has meant that clients of investment managers and financial advisors must take more risks if they are to achieve their income objectives, match their liabilities, or make good on the promises they have made to stakeholders. They will be prepared to take these risks only if a trusted partner accompanies them. Managers and advisors must therefore do more to build trust by conveying warmth. Without trust, some of the economic consequences that have become familiar in recent years – like public and regulatory disdain for the financial services industry, and the stellar growth of robo-products and robo-services – might also persist.

WHAT WE FOUND OUT ON THE WAY

It would be practical to have a list of simple recommendations for winning trust, but this is not possible – all clients are different and so are all asset managers. However, there are some client goals that service providers must aim to satisfy, as they consistently reappear in the emergence and building of trust.

Be trustworthy for me

Fund clients certainly know that past performance is not a guarantee of future performance. Its role in asset manager selection decisions owes more to agency issues than to any belief in its predictive power. They probably know, too, that non-performance factors are not useful predictors of future performance either, at least not in the way that they are often employed. So why do they look at them (and why do academic researchers look at them looking at them)? It is because selection decisions are not primarily about future performance. Clients have a relationship with investment managers in which they are vulnerable. So they focus on the factors that will inform them about what that relationship will be like. Of course, they want capable individuals, and past performance data says something about a manager's ability to achieve desirable outcomes. However, the primary concern is about the manager's *intentions*. Is the manager motivated to devote that ability to pursuing desirable outcomes for the client, or for himself? Only when the manager is judged favourably on the warmth and competence dimensions will he be trusted. Trust is not about predicting future performance, it is about predicting what will happen in the relationship for any given future scenario.

Be you for me

To make a judgement about whether to trust, clients need to form an impression of the manager. The elements that inform that decision will come mainly from what the manager (and others) says and does, but also from cues in the physical and social environment. Much to the chagrin of managers, many of those elements will have nothing to do with investment philosophy, methodology, innovation or performance. Clients want to discover something about the individuals, and about what makes those people tick. Managers must give them that information, deliberately. If they do not, clients will gather it anyway: from the way the manager looks and dresses; the activities he is engaged in; the networks he frequents; or even the behavioural residue he leaves in his office when he is not there. It is not manipulation to show other people who we really are, as long as we do it honestly. This is preferable to allowing chance, or an outdated stereotype, to convey an inaccurate picture.

Care for me

Clients want to be cared for. They want to be cherished members of a privileged in-group, 'one of us', part of the family, because families care for their own. Hence, they look for signs of a family resemblance in their service providers – for instance, in their values, preferences, priorities and other similarities. Managers whose values genuinely overlap with those of a prospective client – which is more common than it sounds – have a clear advantage. Yet clients do not always make the discovery of their values and priorities easy. They sometimes struggle to verbalise them, or feel ill at ease doing so. Sometimes, when they do express their values, managers do not notice because they are not actively listening.

Managers must do the work to identify areas of value congruence with clients, and use these perspectives and attitudes in their communication. Framing arguments and recommendations in values that are alien to the counterparty will result in ineffective communication. Managers must also learn to listen to what clients say. Active listening means paying one's entire attention to what the other is saying – not thinking simultaneously about other things, or planning what one is going to say as soon as the other has stopped talking. In doing so they not only gain insights into clients' values, they also demonstrate that clients enjoy a privileged position.

Do something

Clients want to have a high-trust relationship with their managers, and vice versa. Each party will draw advantages from such a relationship, both on an interpersonal level, and possibly on an interorganisational level too. This is a genuine win-win situation. The only 'drawback' is that it is the manager who must do all of the work to bring such a relationship about. This might explain why efforts in this direction are often so timid, despite the advantages. Service providers should start by doing something, anything. Once one makes some effort to convey warmth, one starts to see how much emotions and behaviour are influenced by our impressions of others – and identifies opportunities to influence it. Every client contact is an opportunity to convey warmth.

ANNEX 1

TRUST GAMES

T O MEASURE THE presence and degree of trust behaviour between two individuals, at least where money is concerned, it is common to use a laboratory experiment known as a trust game.[126] There are several versions of this experiment, but the basic two-stage structure is the following:

A trust game involves two anonymously paired experimental subjects. The experimenter awards the first a monetary sum – say, $50. That person (the sender, or trustor) is then invited to share some, all, or none of the amount with the second subject (the receiver, or trustee). The experimenter agrees to triple whatever amount is shared. The receiver is then invited to return some, all, or none of the new amount with the sender. Although collusion is not allowed, both experimental subjects are aware of the rules of the game in advance. They are also aware that the only way to maximise the total monetary reward is to cooperate fully. If the sender gives the entire sum to the receiver the maximum bonus will be earned. The new amount could then be equitably

---

126 Berg, J., Dickhaut, J. and McCabe, K. (1995) 'Trust, reciprocity, and social history'. *Games and Economic Behavior*, 10 (1), 122–142.

shared between the pair. Both parties would walk away with $75 in this case. However, to achieve this outcome, the sender must run the risk of the receiver simply pocketing the shared amount, and the bonus, and disappearing into the mist. In other words, the sender must believe the receiver is trustworthy before sharing anything. The amount sent in a trust game is therefore considered to reflect trust, and the amount returned a measure of trustworthiness.

Some critics have raised doubts as to whether the trust game is really measuring trust and not some other social phenomenon, like altruism. So, it is with scientific reserve that we continue to use the expression 'trust' to describe the results of these experiments. However, the popularity of the approach among trust researchers has, at least, meant it has been frequently replicated in many countries around the world. It has also been tried using subjects of varying ages, a variety of monetary amounts and bonuses, and counterparties who have had some information about each other revealed to each other in advance. Thus it has yielded a wealth of data.

TRUST AROUND THE WORLD

Despite the economic risks involved in handing over part of one's endowment to a stranger they will never meet or see, in the hope that this anonymous counterparty returns the favour, trustors do it quite frequently. And trustees, although they have nothing to gain economically from returning money to the trustor in the second stage of the game, are quite prone to making a generous gesture. Indeed, the more money trustors send, the more trustees seem to reciprocate. Consequently, the best strategy for the trustor is to risk everything and send the entire endowment. The second-best strategy is to give nothing at all. Attempts by trustors to 'hedge their bets' by sending only small amounts, tend to attract a jaundiced response from trustees. Such expressions of partial trust tend not to encourage reciprocity and therefore reduce trustors' final outcomes.

In data from one meta-study[127] of trust games across the world, the average proportion of the initial endowment sent was approximately half. In some countries, average proportions sent were as high as 70%. Receivers were not as generous but they too returned on average more than a third of the final endowment. These averages hide a considerable amount of variability in the proportions sent and returned, of course. But they are nonetheless remarkable, in that they are significantly different from zero. People are motivated to trust and to reciprocate trusting behaviour with trustworthiness.

---

127 Johnson, N. D. and Mislin, A. A. (2011) 'Trust games: A meta-analysis'. *Journal of Economic Psychology*, 32, 865–889.

Country	Number of studies	Total sample size	Average proportion sent	Average proportion returned
Argentina	3	678	0.43	0.40
Australia	2	196	0.51	0.32
Austria	6	508	0.62	0.38
Bangladesh	4	863	0.46	0.46
Brazil	2	138	0.71	0.45
Bulgaria	2	62	0.57	0.39
Cameroon	2	320	0.70	0.47
Canada	5	432	0.60	0.31
China	5	1036	0.48	0.55
Colombia	2	722	0.37	0.23
Costa Rica	1	425	0.46	0.26
France	9	1008	0.43	0.33
Germany	15	1315	0.51	0.44
Honduras	1	758	0.49	0.42
Hungary	1	74	0.51	0.40
India	1	92	0.49	0.29
Israel	2	535	0.59	0.45
Italy	8	763	0.43	0.31
Japan	2	78	0.58	0.32
Kenya	4	646	0.38	0.32
Netherlands	6	751	0.46	0.33
New Zealand	2	123	0.44	0.22
Paraguay	1	188	0.47	0.43
Peru	2	1245	0.48	0.46
Russia	2	758	0.49	0.37
South Africa	4	775	0.44	0.24
South Korea	1	52	0.67	0.29
Sweden	4	941	0.74	0.37

Switzerland	1	986	0.66	0.53
Tanzania	2	310	0.54	0.4
Uganda	2	246	0.45	0.33
United Kingdom	5	274	0.54	0.28
United States	46	4552	0.51	0.34
Uruguay	1	579	0.45	0.29
Vietnam	2	194	0.33	n/a

Source: Johnson, N. D. and Mislin, A. A. (2011).

INDEX

D

E

F

S

V

W

Z